LONELY

A Collection of Poetry and Prose
on Loneliness and Being Alone

Compiled by Robin Barratt

With...

Abigail George, Alan Murphy, Alan Rorke, Alistair Baptista, Anna Cheung, Ashraf Booley, Bernard Levinson. Cameron John Bryce, Chandra Gurung, Charmane MacGregor, Christine Mcleod, Claudia Hardt, Courtney Speedy, David Hollywood, Dawa Rinzin, Douglas Bruton, Farha A. Jaleel, Gail Dendy, Gayathri Viswanath, Grace Ebbey, Guy Morris, Heidi Al Khajah, Ian McKenzie, Irwin Rego, James Scalise, J D Trejo-Maya, Karishma Krishna Kumar, Kathleen Boyle, Keith Nunes, Lonita Nugrahayu, Lucy Reid, Lynda Chouiten, Lynda Jessen-Tye, Lynda Tavakoli, Madhavi Dwivedi, Maire Malone, Maren Bodenstein, Margaret Clough, Mary Burgerhout, Megan Macleod, Nilanjana Bose, Omar Ahmed, Robert Hirschfield, Rohini Sunderam, Rosie Mapplebeck, Ryan Joel, Sally Spedding, Sameer Qamar, Sara Spivey, Shirley Sampson, Simon Atkin, Simon Wong, Stu Armstrong, Toni Curran, Tyrrel Francis, Vaijayantee Bhattacharya and *Zahra Zuhair.*

Published by Robin Barratt
© Robin Barratt 2016 and all the authors herein

All rights reserved. No part of this publication may be reproduced,
distributed, or transmitted in any form or by any means,
including photocopying, recording, or other electronic or mechanical methods,
without the prior written permission of the publisher,
except in the case of brief quotations embodied in critical reviews and
certain other non-commercial uses permitted by copyright law.
For permission requests, email the publisher at the address below.

W: www.collectionsofpoetryandprose.com
E: Robin@collectionsofpoetryandprose.com
E: RobinBarratt@yahoo.com

Special Thanks To...

The Bahrain Writers' Circle (www.BahrainWritersCircle.com) Pen South Africa (www.pensouthafrica.co.za), South African Writers College (www.sawriterscollege.co.za), New Zealand Writers' College (www.nzwriterscollege.co.nz), the Scottish Poetry Library (www.scottishpoetrylibrary.org.uk), Huntly Writers, Aberdeenshire, Scotland (www.huntlywriters.co.uk) Scottish Book Trust (www.scottishbooktrust.com), Poets House. New York, USA (www.PoetsHouse.org), Literature Wales (www.literaturewales.org), Lismore Poetry Group, Donny O'Rourke's Barrington Bards poetry group in Glasgow and The London Writers' Cafe, some of whose poets and writers contributed to this book after notices were kindly sent out to their members. Thank you!

Contents By Title...

Introduction by Robin Barratt. Page 09

Listen Carefully by Lonita Nugrahayu. Page 12
Empty Chair by Lynda Jessen-Tye. Page 15
A Wooden Heart by Douglas Bruton. Page 16
Solitude by Rohini Sunderam. Page 18
Not There by Mary Burgerhout. Page 19
One Day In Spring by Kathleen Boyle. Page 20
The Ladder by Anna Cheung. Page 22
An Ode For Soulace by Irwin Rego. Page 23
As I Sit Alone by Tyrrel Francis. Page 24
Company by Lynda Chouiten. Page 25
But I Loved You All The Same by Courtney Speedy. Page 26
Just Breathe by Heidi Al Khajah. Page 29
Loneliness by Margaret Clough. Page 30
Tokai by Bernard Levinson. Page 31
Briefcase by Shirley Sampson. Page 36
Ring A Ring Of Roses, A Pocketful Of Posies.... by Rosie Mapplebeck. Page 37
Darren Unlearns Loneliness At The Old Country Inn by Alistair Baptista. Page 38
Gone by Gail Dendy. Page 40
Brother by Keith Nunes. Page 41
My Lover, Loneliness by Megan Macleod. Page 42
Anticipatory Nostalgia For Loneliness by Abigail George. Page 43
Depression by Ashraf Booley. Page 46
The Arrangement by Karishma Krishna Kumar. Page 47
Bereft by Rohini Sunderam. Page 49
Apart by James Scalise. Page 50
Cruise by Sally Spedding. Page 51
That Special Little Boy by Courtney Speedy. Page 52
Coffee by Simon Wong. Page 54
Losing Myself by Dilraz AR Kunnummal. Page 56
A Small Measure Of Peace by Sameer Qamar. Page 58
The Old Fisherman And The Country by Chandra Gurung. Page 59
I Am by Gail Dendy. Page 61
Waiting Spaces by David Hollywood. Page 62
Loneliness by Lonita Nugrahayu. Page 63
Alone by Omar Ahmed. Page 64
Sharing The Journey by Shirley Sampson. Page 65
Alone by Farha A. Jaleel. Page 66
The Bag Lady by Maire Malone. Page 67

The Hole by Claudia Hardt. Page 68
Salt by Grace Ebbey. Page 70
Out Of Africa And Into A Sea Of Discomfort by Keith Nunes. Page 71
Lost by Charmane MacGregor. Page 72
Finding Yourself Lost by Cameron John Bryce. Page 73
Loneliness by Vaijayantee Bhattacharya. Page 74
Nobody by Simon Atkin. Page 75
Bloody Valentine by Courtney Speedy. Page 76
Open Window by Alan Murphy. Page 77
One Night Stand by Karishma Krishna Kumar. Page 78
Happiness by Stu Armstrong. Page 79
Summer Days At The Mt. Eden by Robert Hirschfield. Page 81
Is This What I Do? by Lynda Tavakoli. Page 82
Love Reunited by Christine Mcleod. Page 83
A Deadening Limbo Of Desuetude by Rohini Sunderam. Page 84
Forgive Me by Lucy Reid. Page 85
Where To Now by David Hollywood. Page 86
Decay by Ryan Joel. Page 87
Love Comes by James Scalise. Page 88
The Failures Of Success by Sameer Qamar. Page 89
Pantoum Of Loneliness by Simon Wong. Page 91
Limewood by Gail Dendy. Page 92
A Million Empty Words by Zahra Zuhair Page 93
Solitude by Lonita Nugrahayu. Page 95
The Solitary Warriors by Irwin Rego. Page 96
Unconnected Senses Sought, Hopeless Depression by David Hollywood. Page 97
Connected by Courtney Speedy. Page 98
Being Alone by Toni Curran. Page 99
Online by Sameer Qamar. Page 101
Forgotten Me by Simon Atkin. Page 103
In Praise Of Dambudzo Marechera's Loneliness by Abigail George. Page 104
In The Dark by Farha A. Jaleel. Page 106
Gone by J D Trejo-Maya. Page 107
The World Turns Around Me by Lynda Chouiten. Page 108
Strays by Ian McKenzie. Page 109
Life Two by Stu Armstrong. Page 110
Grasping by Heidi Al Khajah. Page 111
Dad by Maire Malone. Page 112
Kitchen Comforts by Lynda Tavakoli. Page 113
My Uncle Don by Keith Nunes. Page 114
Alone In My Head by Megan MacLeod. Page 116
I Sat On Your Lap by Courtney Speedy. Page 117

Back by Shirley Sampson. Page 119
Cocaine by Courtney Speedy. Page 120
Why? By Stu Armstrong. Page 121
The Deserted Beach by Gail Dendy. Page 123
Solitary Confinement by Nilanjana Bose. Page 124
Hollow As A Fallen Echo by Irwin Rego. Page 126
Death, Love, Hate, Blood by Stu Armstrong. Page 127
Sightless Loneliness by David Hollywood. Page 129
Fatal Attraction by Ryan Joel. Page 130
Beyond Strength by Heidi Al Khajah. Page 132
What Could Be More Romantic by James Scalise. Page 133
Alone by Karishma Krishna Kumar. Page 135
Acres I Imagine by Cameron John Bryce. Page 136
Under The Bed Wallowing by Keith Nunes. Page 137
Missing You by Rohini Sunderam. Page 138
Away by Shirley Sampson. Page 139
Addiction by Courtney Speedy. Page 140
A Lonely Heart by Rosie Mapplebeck. Page 142
Seven Minutes by Sara Spivey. Page 143
Loneliness by Madhavi Dwivedi. Page 145
Puppy Pees On The Lawn by Maren Bodenstein. Page 146
A Direct Hit by Alan Murphy. Page 147
The Truth He Tried To Tell Me by Keith Nunes. Page 148
Sharp! by Abigail George. Page 149
Melancholy by Ryan Joel. Page 151
Can I Walk Alongside? by Charmane MacGregor. Page 153
Loneliness by Megan Macleod. Page 153
The Disregarded Town by Simon Wong. Page 154
Trauma by Gail Dendy. Page 155
Loneliness by Guy Morris. Page 157
Jigsaw Blues by Cameron John Bryce. Page 158
Whenever You Behold by James Scalise. Page 159
Indifference Of A Tree by Alan Rorke. Page 160
Silent Prayers by Karishma Krishna Kumar. Page 161
Smoking by Simon Atkin. Page 163
Loneliness At Work by Dawa Rinzin. Page 161
All Alone by Gayathri Viswanath. Page 165
Hello, Goodbye by Rohini Sunderam. Page 166

Contributors' Biographies. Page 167

Contents By Author...

Abigail George. Pages 43, 104, 149
Alan Murphy. Pages 77, 147
Alan Rorke. Page 160
Alistair Baptista. Page 38
Anna Cheung. Page 22
Ashraf Booley. Page 46
Bernard Levinson. Page 31
Cameron John Bryce. Pages 73, 136, 158
Chandra Gurung. Page 59
Charmane MacGregor. Pages 72, 153
Christine Mcleod. Page 83
Claudia Hardt. Page 68
Courtney Speedy. Pages 26, 52, 76, 98, 117, 120, 140
David Hollywood. Pages 62, 86, 97, 129
Dawa Rinzin. Page 161
Douglas Bruton. Page 16
Farha A. Jaleel. Pages 66, 106
Gail Dendy. Pages 40, 61, 92, 123, 155
Gayathri Viswanath. Page 165
Grace Ebbey. Page 70
Guy Morris. Page 157
Heidi Al Khajah. Pages 29, 111, 132
Ian McKenzie. Page 109
Irwin Rego. Pages 23, 96, 126
James Scalise. Pages 50, 28, 133, 159
J D Trejo-Maya. Page 107
Kathleen Boyle. Page 20
Karishma Krishna Kumar. Pages 47, 78, 135, 161
Keith Nunes. Pages 41, 71, 114, 137, 148
Lonita Nugrahayu. Pages 12, 63, 95
Lucy Reid. Page 85
Lynda Chouiten. Pages 25, 108
Lynda Jessen-Tye. Page 15
Lynda Tavakoli. Pages 82, 113
Madhavi Dwivedi. Page 145
Maire Malone. Pages 67, 112
Maren Bodenstein. Page 146
Margaret Clough. Page 30
Mary Burgerhout. Page 19
Megan Macleod. Pages 42, 116, 153
Nilanjana Bose. Page 124
Omar Ahmed. Page 64

Robert Hirschfield. Page 81
Rohini Sunderam. Pages 18, 49, 84, 138, 166
Rosie Mapplebeck. Pages 37, 142
Ryan Joel. Pages 87, 130, 151
Sally Spedding. Page 51
Sameer Qamar. Pages 58, 89, 101
Sara Spivey. Page 143
Shirley Sampson. Pages 36, 65, 119, 139
Simon Atkin. Pages 75, 103, 168
Simon Wong. Pages 54, 91, 154
Stu Armstrong. Pages 79, 110, 121, 127
Toni Curran. Page 99
Tyrrel Francis. Page 24
Vaijayantee Bhattacharya. Page 74
Zahra Zuhair. Page 93

Introduction
By Robin Barratt

I am not a poet. Writing poetry and short prose, for me anyway, I find extremely difficult and undeniably challenging. I can write fairly lengthy non-fiction prose with relative ease and, over the years, have written a large number of books, from true crime and sport to travel and biography, but I struggle finding my creative mind, and struggle even further putting that often vague and wispy creativity into a meaningful and stimulating poetic or short prose context. However, saying that, I do thoroughly enjoy reading poetry and short prose, and am always both inspired and fascinated by the way writers can summarise their thoughts, feelings and emotions into just a few carefully selected, carefully structured and amazingly significant words and sentences. For me, this skill is truly magical.

Why a book on the subject of loneliness and being alone? Because, whether we admit it to ourselves or not, and no matter what sort of lives we have led, or are leading, most of us at some point have felt, or feel, lonely or alone. And of course, everyone's experience of loneliness differs. So, with this in mind, I thought I'd put together a collection on this poignant, touching and often painful subject, whilst showcasing the work of some amazing writers and poets around the world. Plus, it is a subject that fascinates me too!

There are 118 contributions from 57 writers in 26 countries, with many of the contributions reflecting the diverse backgrounds and cultures of the writers. Writing poetry is an extremely individual and personal process, with few (if any) rules and regulations, and so I have kept almost every contribution exactly as sent, regardless of structure, punctuation and capitalisation. This is the poet's work, and not mine to alter! I have also accepted almost every piece of work sent, regardless of the contributors' skill and experience; my ambitions are to see writers' work published and read, and certainly not to judge, critique or criticize. I have thoroughly enjoyed the naive and simple just as much as the more complex and profound. Focusing on just about every aspect of loneliness and being alone, and covering topics as diverse as old age, bereavement, abandonment, divorce, entrapment, unrequited love, depression, trauma, failure and addiction, as well as the more abstract and esoteric; LONELY is being acclaimed worldwide for its diversity and mix of writers and styles.

I hope you enjoy this little book as much as I have enjoyed putting it together, and if you want to know a little more about any of the writers featured, there is a short biography of most of them at the end of the book. And if you like writing and like having your words published and read, then we have more wonderful Collections planned for publishing, so do contribute. Details at the back of this book.

Best wishes and ENJOY!!

Robin Barratt
Editor and Publisher
E: RobinBarratt@yahoo.com

LONELY

A Collection of Poetry and Prose
on Loneliness and Being Alone

Listen Carefully
By Lonita Nugrahayu

Have you ever listened carefully to silence, my dear?
If you do,
would you agree with me that it is the noisiest noise you could ever hear.
It really is.

In silence,
I could hear my loudest cry,
even though I may have no rains on my face.

In silence,
I could hear my terrifying scream,
even though I never scream before.

In silence,
I could hear all the noises behind my smiles.

Don't you hear them, too, my dear?
I doubt you do.
Because if you hear them,
you would be hugging me tight by now.

Do you think I am crazy,
for painting smile on my face in the middle of chaotic mind, a bleeding heart, and a broken soul?
Do you think I should let everyone sees my transparent stitches of my wounded self?
But my dear,
aren't we all supposed to smile,
no matter what happen inside us?

I guess I smile beautifully then,
it delusions everybody
that even those stay close to me,
fail to see the storm behind my smiles.

What about my eyes?
I heard eyes are window to our soul.
Could you see my soul reflected on them, dear?

But oh silly me,

how could you see them?
as I fancy those big trendy sunglasses to cover them up.

My friends love my shades,
they praise them all the time.
I am not sure though,
if they still do praise them if I take off my shades.
Because then,
you and them could see how wonderfully he paints colors of blue or purple on my eyes.
The eyes that was once a upon a time,
got sparkly stars on them.

He's an excellent make up artist, isn't he?
like a magician,
who could vanish stars in the blink of an eye.

Perhaps he could be an excellent make up artist.
But wait,
no dear... it would be terrible,
as his eye shadows palette come with pains,
physically and emotionally.
But I am so in love, my dear...
that I hide my pains behind these trendy sunglasses and smiles.
Is it love, by the way...
or stupidity?
You name it, my dear,
to me...
it is loneliness.

I know you must be blaming me,
everyone will do,
that I let myself carry the pains,
alone and for a long time.

But dear,
I have lost trust.
I thought I am surrounded by those who are genuinely care for me.
Because if they do,
they woukd see the sorrows that have been reflected on me.

Ah,
I guess I smile beautifully then.
And I guess,
nobody is genuinely caring for me.

But this silence, dear...
it cares for me.
It could listen
to all misery and sorrows that you and everybody fail to listen.
The silence could understand
the silent silence of loneliness
that gradually shutting off the smiles,
and let it dies alongside the soul that I once owned.

Empty Chair
By Lynda Jessen-Tye

I sit in the chair
that you used to sit in
and it brings me comfort -
almost as if you are with me still.

But then I remember that you've gone
and it's just me in this big old house now.
And the cat.

A Wooden Heart
By Douglas Bruton

He has a small brown suitcase he takes with him everywhere: in the car on long journeys; on the bus into town; carried to the shop at the end of the street whenever he needs a quarter ounce of Ogden's Redbreast Flake tobacco for his pipe. The suitcase is old, the stiffened corners battered and scraped. Fading travel stickers cover one side, reminders of where he has been – where *they* have been. Always with the one suitcase; to Morecombe, Blackpool, and Edinburgh. To St Ives in sunnier days.

Once, he went over to Paris. Years back. There was a reason for going, but he does not think of that now. He remembers smoking his Kaywoodie pipe sitting on a bench in the Tuileries Gardens, the sun on his face, the air sweetened by something, and a sculpture by Aristide Maillol that made him want to laugh – it was of a woman as thick as a tree and as heavy.

In the Gardens he watched a puppet show telling the story of lost or unrequited love. The strings of the puppets were soon invisible and he became so wrapped up in the story it made him cry; a young girl in a summer dress, ribbons in her hair, pointed and said something to her mama, and the woman pulled her daughter quickly away.

Now, he just travels into town and back, or over to his sister's on Sundays for lunch. Always the suitcase goes with him. Used to be people'd ask about it, why he was never without it. They thought he might be a travelling salesman, the suitcase holding samples of what he had to sell – ladies' perfume, or silk handkerchiefs in all colours, or watches bearing the names of distinction. He told them the suitcase contained a change of clothes: a suit, a fresh shirt and clean socks. 'Just in case,' he said, laughing at his own joke, the laughter diverting attention away from the suitcase. No one asks anymore, or even notices.

When he's alone, curtains drawn, the door to his room shut and locked, he lays the suitcase on a bed or a table, flicks the catches, lifts the lid. Inside is a doll, a stringless wooden puppet-girl dressed in old lace and with her hair loose. Her name's Emily. He lifts her out of the case, gentle as though she's blood and breath, and he sits her on his knee. He fixes her hair, the folds of her dress. Then he takes one small wooden hand in his and he tells Emily about his day, where he's been, where *they've* been. And he tells her what he's seen and heard and felt. He tells her everything, and Emily listens as only wood or stone can listen, patient and unresponsive. As he talks, he strokes the back of her wooden hand, and the smoke from his pipe sweetens the air in the room, and he cries again, like that day in the Tuileries Gardens in Paris.

Solitude
By Rohini Sunderam

Such solitariness I have known
Total. Complete.
The satisfaction of being myself
And me alone.
The breezes were my playmates
The rains were made for me
Who else had I need for
And who had need for me?

But then a yearning filled me
Strange and hitherto
Alien to my soul.
A disturbing thrashing around of my spirit.
I searched
I called
I wept
To the unfeeling skies above me
Surely, somewhere
There was someone else like me!

This solitariness I too have known
That I live and die
Alone.

Not There
By Mary Burgerhout

The solemn rituals of death are past
And family and friends now step away.
As solitude unchecked beckons at last
I face the first of many lonely days.
I wander through each room, forever changed
Yet with a thousand memories of you
And contemplate a future – frightening, strange
Without my love, my life, to see it through.
And oh! the coming home from work to find
All as it was when morning saw me leave
Not there to move a teacup, close the blind
Not there, the aching void left unrelieved.
We, fallible, must bear a two-edged cross
The fleeting joy of love, the pain of loss.

One Day in Spring
By Kathleen Boyle

There were days Joan wondered if she were a ghost; days she would awaken to the usual sounds of morning, the ticking clock, dripping tap, birdsong, but there was nobody to notice. She would linger in bed until her body stirred.

Once, when she was young and troubled by the stress of heartbreak, she woke in the night and found that, sitting up in bed, she had left her body behind. Alarmed, she watched herself, a tousle of dark curls on the pillow, then stared into the darkness of her room, wondering what would happen if she walked away. 'I'd better get back.' she thought, and lying down, became as one.

Today, no longer young, she heaved her aching joints from bed and steadying her fragile frame moved forward to begin another day. She sighed, opening the wardrobe and choosing yellow; 'Nice for the spring,' she thought.

Breakfasting on tea and toast at the little table in the bay window of her magnolia living room, she watched the children passing on their way to school and thought about her own three, and the years of morning chaos as they began their day. 'When did it all end?' She mused. 'When was our last frantic family dash to get away from home?'

She took the bus out of the village and into town, with no other reason but to pass the time. She often did. Wandering, 'Like a lost soul', her mother would have said. A ghost, unseen by the bustling hoards in whom she saw herself, at one time or another over the years, school girls, lovers, mothers. The memories were legion. And then there were the other ghosts, the white haired lonely remnants of lives which had, too soon, passed by. They sometimes said hello and she would respond in kind. 'I suppose to verify that we exist.' She told herself.

Rising slowly from the bench, her regular pausing place in the Cathedral's shadow, Joan acknowledged that this day, with its puffs of white cloud drifting high above the little town, the intermittent sunshine brightening pink blossomed trees and crocus strewn grass verges, was a different day, for she had felt a tightening of her chest at breakfast time, and spasms on and off throughout the day. She timed them, as she had timed contractions on the days her babies came.

On the bus home she marvelled at the trees in bud, recalling, with some sadness, their summer loveliness.

It was a struggle to reach the top of the stairs and she thought, whimsically, of the mountains she had climbed in her youth. There was a moment of ecstasy as the bed took the weight of her exhausted body, a final agony and sleep.

Sitting up in bed, she slipped her feet to the floor, then looking down, saw herself, white hair tousled on the pillow, peaceful. Pain free, she stood and stepped away into the dark.

The Ladder
By Anna Cheung

Stepping up the rungs of the ladder,
he ascends the spinal column of age.
With every step, the wooden joints
groan under the weight of his heart,
With every step, the rungs creak from
the sigh which blows from his lips.
The ladder rattles against the silence
that hangs from his skeletal memories

Stepping up the rungs of the ladder,
he ascends the spinal column of age.
With every step, the sheen on his hair
rusts to grey and his spectacles blur in vision.
With every step, the crease between his brows
deepen and his gums recede into his hollow face.
Yet he cannot stop, he cannot rest
until he reaches the topmost rung of the ladder.

An Ode For Soulace
By Irwin Rego

As babies, we arrive, pure and pristine - souls from the oceans of sincerity
Only to be polluted by the sands of norms and the anfractuosities
We walk the shores adhering to teachings thrust upon us
Instructed, the rules in the harbor are sacrosanct, accept it – the mattering truth buzz!

Meanwhile on land, the game players and politicians thrive with their deceit and balderdash tonality
An unargumentative crowd follows, opinionated but refusing to be typecast as herd mentality.
Whilst the game of power, control, ego continues - spreading the acrimony
Religions propagated on pedestals - ours is better than yours - a slap on the face of intelligence and harmony
Ethnicity, Caste, Colour prejudice – you ponder when and where did it get its malevolent wings
Sexual Orientation, gender discrimination – and the fat lady still sings!

Time being short, we forget our intelligence has evolved with our learning.
We query, comprehend, debate all this mess, still not sure of our leaning
Our sense of self along with the ego meanwhile taking precedence over everything in question
The Good Samaritan, a noble tale we preach - in reality, all highfalutin

Maybe, we have all forgotten to live, as we with our pride and airs fend
Existing by making it a lifeless journey towards a monotonous end
The kaleidoscope of fun, freedom and wholesomeness, as babies we had – maybe time for stimulation
For Real SOULace is awakening the forgotten true self within – that elusive jubilation!

As I Sit Alone
By Tyrrel Francis

As I sit alone, without you here with me
I did not know, just how hard this would be
I keeps the scars, and hold them dear
To keep you in my heart so near
I learn to live without regret
To cherish you, and not forget.

I wait my turn, until I see
Where you went, when you left me
I feel until then, your presence near
And what I'd do, to have you here
I hold the day we meet again
In my heart, to ease the strain.

Company
By Lynda Chouiten

No I was not alone
There were plenty around
With voices that resound
And laughter in the air.
No I was not alone
They were quite many
Rather good company
Except they were not there.

Good, company, I said?
Not so sure, after all.
Conversing with a wall –
And walls do have their moods –
Is not good for your head.
A wall can send you hate
Or want to be your... mate
Or be awfully rude.

But I Loved You All The Same
By Courtney Speedy

I'm not trying to sound poetic intentionally, I'm really not. It's just I can still smell you on my pillows and in my skin. Is this what letting the devil win feels like? It's a harsh strike to take, especially when everything I feel now is so fake. I'd give all I have and more to see you standing by the door. You were my morning coffee and late night smoke, you held me when the demons awoke and the world shook as I screamed and felt my heart rip at the seams.

You had red hair down to your waist and a sweet sultry smile that made me wonder what you knew. I would watch you draw and paint so effortlessly and elegant and never once did you go over the lines. You smelt of sunshine and perfume but hated the rain and the way I had long baths. I loved your tattoos that adorned your beautiful body but hated the sad sunken eyes and the dissolvable lies. You didn't have to tell me you were working late again or some other excuse because I know time management caused you to hit the roof. As reckless and ruthless as the day we met when you asked me out for a bet, I thought you would grow out of it like an old pair of jeans except you never did so I dropped the subject of wanting kids.

I planted a garden out back one summer and came home one day after work to see soil and dug up roots all over the lawn. When I asked you what the hell had happened you just faked a yawn and went to bed. I had always known you weren't right in the head; you would be in the kitchen talking to yourself at 4 in the morning and you weren't even yawning. Sleep didn't like you and you weren't that fond of it either, you were either up for 4 days at a time or in bed sleepily mumbling a rhyme.

Bipolar suited you perfectly, it was all you had ever known but refused diagnosis instead calling them "spells." They were the kind of spells that put me through hell because there was only so much I could do before you got cruel. I know you never meant the words you said but I still replay them in my head. You were so beautiful but broken that night and it seemed to fit you distressingly well. You had tried to claw the phone out of my hand that night you snapped. 55kgs of manic madness may not seem like much but I feared for my life for the first time then. Your eyes were flitting around the room seeing fictional things and you ripped off your wedding ring. I later found it under the bed and put it in your drawers by your bed for when you'd come back to collect your belongings - except you never did.

It took two police officers to restrain you that night and it pained me indefinitely to see a skeleton of my wife pinned on the ground. I'm sorry I saw reality when you saw delusions and I'm sorry I never saw the warning signs because you were so far from fine. I come and visit you once a week for a couple of hours which I like. Most of the time you just listen to me talk about work and mundane things like that because you miss being out in this high speed city we live in. Last time I came to see you you were learning how to knit and had made dozens of brightly coloured scarves. You seemed ignorantly happy which was much better than before. I wanted to hold your hand but you flinched whenever I tried to touch you. You wrapped one of your scarves around my neck as I was leaving the hospital and asked if I could bring you your old sketch book. So I took it with me this morning to give to you. But you weren't in your ward. They said you had had another episode and were now sleeping it off. I asked to see you and I could see the sympathy in the nurse's face as she realised I was your husband and you were my wife except now it was a lonely life.

You were sleeping so peacefully with your beautiful red hair fanned out around you. I tried to ignore the cuffs that chained your left wrist to the bed and instead focused on your face. You used to love wearing make-up so much that I hardly saw you without it but now I was seeing the real raw beauty of yours you had tried so hard to hide. I put your sketch book on the bedside dresser and kissed your limp hand whilst wondering why you looked so bland.
You didn't stir at all and I wondered what you were dreaming of. I wondered if you missed me or if you weren't even able to comprehend what we were anymore?

So I'll drive home alone now and have a smoke or two outside as the sun begins to hide. Tomorrow is another day and although your insanity robbed you of normality, it didn't rob you of me. You'll always have my heart even though I have moved on and met somebody new; she isn't you and perhaps that's the best and worst thing all at the same time. It was a different kind of love you and I had, it was reckless and wild but you had the mentality of a child. The words we said at the altar have a different meaning to them now but it's alright and it's okay because I promised I would always stay.

I can still smell you on my pillow and taste you in my morning coffee but it's quiet now in the house. No more hiding the knives and hearing hollowed cries; the only aches and pains I hear now are the ones inside of my head. I miss you Red. This lifetime feels so dull now that your vibrance has gone. You were my morning coffee and late night smoke. You were my shot of energy and insanity. Fuck, you were even the cavity in my tooth and the maniac idiot dancing on the roof.

You were insane but I loved you all the same.

Just Breathe
By Heidi Al Khajah

I will breathe
I will not be afraid
I will start to begin again
I will be forceful
With gumption
Why is it that we fear?
What is it that calls us to those depths?

Breathe easy my love
Breathe easy for me
I am the calm in the night
I am the one that stops the storms
You have no fear
No dread for
I am by you r side always
Now do what I do
Put your palm against mine
Clasp our hands
And we shall be forever

Loneliness
By Margaret Clough

I wake and stretch my feet down, spread my arms
to touch the boundaries of my narrow bed.
I find no reason to get up, and yet
I rise, brush hair and teeth. I dress.

I hold a book that I have read before.
My fingers, as they turn a page,
can feel the emptiness between the lines.

In the next room, a radio drones on
talks, quiz shows, plays and newscasts
all disperse unheard in stagnant air.

Outside my window in the road, I see
an old dog waddling round and round.
Head up to sniff, he drops his tail;
his ears droop down.

I sit at table in a dusty room,
a newspaper beside my plate.
I don't sweep up the crumbs
or put my cup away.
I have stopped listening for the phone to ring.

Tokai
By Bernard Levinson

Looking back on that night, a sense of timelessness stands out. And a profound exhaustion. On my knees at the side of her bed, my hand locked in her womb, I had to nudge the seconds with my own heartbeats. It seems to me now that from the moment I was woken by the constable, time had geared itself into slow motion.

"It's the Bezuidenhouts. The baby's coming..."

I drove for an eternity in the darkness of the Tokai forest looking for their home. Endless black tree-tunnels and railway cottages asleep behind the thick blanket bush in the folds of Muizenberg mountain. But none with lights on. At moments I could see the mountain face against the dark sky. Then a sudden clearing and in my headlights – rows of grapevines' arms outstretched, crucified on the supporting wood, the white gables of an old farm homestead and, immediately, trees again, their heads bent together in the darkness.

I recall the feeling of excitement and fear I always had going on a 'call'. An eager anticipation – and at the very core of this eagerness, a strange dread. Always in equal proportions – my haste to arrive, to meet this new challenge – and the holding back, the uncertainty and the fear. Somewhere in this fear was the pressure of omnipotence. The need of those in distress to find me certain, all-knowing and magical. I hid my vulnerability in gentleness. My fear imprisoned me. I was never sure if I could fulfill the role I sensed and read, again and again, in the eyes of those who suffered.

It was midnight when Kleinman Bezuidenhout waved me in from the road. I could hear his wife calling – riding the crest of her pain in a loud cry. We hurried into the cottage.

I was immediately struck by the incongruity of Kleinman's name. This was not the childhood sarcasm of the tall boy called Shorty. Kleinman appeared to be short because of the massiveness of his chest and shoulders. The impact was of enormous strength. He was dark-skinned and had a large, drooping moustache. A Spanish touch. An air of brooding and melancholy. A heavy silence.

The cottage was dimly lit. The smell of paraffin and camphor. Mrs Bezuidenhout lay flat on her back, holding the bars of the worn metal bedhead. An old, soiled sheet partly covered her body. She was an enormous woman. Her large breasts had fallen into the hollows of her armpits. They looked tired and collapsed. Her entire body was wet with perspiration. As I walked in, she clearly passed into the trough between contractions. She grunted with each breath, her eyes closed. A tiny baby's hand protruded from the dark cleft between her thighs. For a moment, she looked like a sombre surrealist painting. A baby's hand gingerly exploring the world between two mountainous thighs. My first impulse was to shake this lonely hand and welcome the child to the darkness of Tokai and the great, sleeping forest around us. I gently eased the hand and arm back into the dark cavern. Again the feeling of slow motion. A dream-like sense of endlessly, timelessly fingering the small hand back into her body.

Kleinman arrived with a basin of hot water. He stood silently waiting, his long, powerful arms hanging loose at his sides. I slow-motioned through the act of taking off my jacket, rolling up my sleeves and washing my hands. In this slow trickle of time, Mrs Bezuidenhout floundered out of the troughs again and again, falling on the peaks of her womb's grasp. She was deeply exhausted. It was impossible to reach her. Impossible to help her break her painful straining. She filled the room with her rhythmic grunts and then, gripping the bedhead behind her, she roared her agony into the night.

The head suddenly appeared. The vagina yawned. With time frozen, I tried to steady the baby's head. Mrs Bezuidenhout took a deep breath. The old iron bedstead creaked with her tightening grip. She put her chin down and began to push deep inside her chest.

Slow motion.

Kleinman was standing at the side of her bed, his eyes wide. He leaned forward, touching the bed with his massive hands.

"Druk!"

One word. The only word he spoke that entire night. Shouted out at the one overwhelming moment. It burst out like the deep snap of a heavy rope.

The baby slipped and slithered, half-turning into my cupped hands.

Slow motion. Slow motion. Time-frozen motion of the baby's arms and body stretched, then folding back into legs and joints.

"Don't push! Hold it! Just hold it a moment!"

My voice floated in the dream-motion of cutting the cord. Mrs Bezuidenhout was silent and unhearing. Her arms remained above her head. Her hands open. Her legs had fallen apart, the knees still bent. Her body glistened in the lamplight.

Kleinman stood at the side of the bed, missing nothing. Silent. Watching me handle the baby. Watching his wife in exhaustion, asleep. Her heavy limbs asleep and her sagged breasts asleep. He stood with his arms at his side. Impotent. Waiting.

The after-birth welled out of the darkness, crowned and eased into my hand. A dark, hot river followed – swelling and bursting in painful slow motion. I forced my fist into the torrent, slipping deep into her body. With my left hand pressing down on her abdomen outside, I pushed the loose folds of the womb against my hidden fist. Slowly the warm flow stopped. Slowly.

It was at that point time stopped completely. It shuddered, froze and came to a total standstill. I was on my knees at the side of her bed. My fist locked inside her. Locked and waiting in a timeless vacuum. In a series of excursions, I grabbed at my medical bag. A syringe. Ampoules. Back to the abdomen, finding my fist and locking the womb. My feet were cramped and in spasm. I tried to shift my weight, with little relief. I completed the final excursion with my free left hand and injected her loose thigh.

Kleinman remained at the side of the bed. I could see heavy beads of sweat on his forehead. His eyes were lamps burning the dark pool at my elbow.

My fist swam in a deep throbbing. The slow rhythm slowed through my hand. Hot pulsations blurring the outline of my fist. My own body picked up this ebb and flow. I closed my eyes and entered the pendulum beat, hearing my body ache and strain in time to the slow ripples that flowed from my fist.

Throughout all this endless time, Kleinman stood at my side, silent. Waiting. His wife opened her eyes for a moment. Seemed aware of the force of my hand inside her. Groaned softly once, and slipped back into her tiredness.

I placed my forehead against her wet thigh. The bed was now gently throbbing. The dark corners of the room closed around me. I could feel the night breathing on the cottage walls. In the forest, the moon climbed out of the trees. I saw her face at the window, pulsating softly. I felt the moon walk on the roof of the cottage. I felt the slow undulations as she eased herself back onto the edge of Muizenberg mountain. The mountain throbbed. And the darkness. The walls of the cottage throbbed.

There was a slight shift of tempo. I listened with the fingers of my fist. Unmistakably I heard the womb flutter and shift itself minutely over my fist. Behind the loud, rhythmic ache of my limbs and my body, in the warm darkness, the womb was waking from its sleep. It turned. Twitched. It lightly felt out the crevasses between my clenched fingers. It stretched and gripped. Stretched again and squeezed my fist firmly. I inched my hand out. A secret dialogue between my hand and the womb. My blunt fist – mute and stolid. The womb excited, chattering and intimately pressing and caressing my hand.

In the moment of utter silence when I withdrew my hand completely, the seconds took up the pulsations in my body – and time began to move.

I sat on the floor, trying to waken my body. I was aware of Kleinman still waiting at my side. He had not moved the entire night. I was suddenly aware of how terrifying it must have been for him watching me at my task.

It was morning when I walked into the kitchen. I leaned on the half-door and smelt the wet morning air. The heavy scent of the Tokai forest compounded of damp earth, oak trees and the sharp edge of pine. In a clearing behind the cottage, Kleinman was digging. He had his back to me. I assumed he was about to bury the placenta. There was something in the way he handled the shovel that kept me locked to him. He had a way of slicking the earth to his side; then with a lightning-fast spin of the shovel, it was there, high above his head – pausing a split-second and then slamming it deep into the soil with incredible force – then flowing immediately into the same rhythm again. His legs were apart, his back moving in my sight. Like a dancer repeating his set choreographed piece, he crouched as the shovel plunged into the earth. He twisted his body and arched himself up as though he were about to leap into the air. Then he snapped into the deep crouch, curling his body around the spade.

Two thoughts struck me at once. The first – that this was a professional. That he obviously handled a shovel every day of his working life. It was an extension of his body. He flicked it and spun it over his head with amazing dexterity. The heavy, silent hands that I had been aware of all night long were now singing what was, for Kleinman, a very familiar song. The rhythm was unchanging and beautiful to watch.

The second thought held me rooted to the door. Kleinman was clearly not burying anything. He was already standing thigh-deep in the trench he had dug.

I could see the muscles of his back repeating a pattern of tension under his shirt. His trousers stuck to his wet thighs. He began to dig faster. The shovel cut deeply into the hole, tearing out a mound of red clay. The clay had hardly settled on the mountain of earth heaping up at Kleinman's side when the shovel snapped back into the trench.

When he stood waist-high in the trench, Kleinman suddenly stopped, stepped out of the hole, took a deep breath – and began digging the earth back into the hole. The same precision. The same professional command of the shovel and the flying clods of earth. He dug furiously. He stood astride the loose earth and remained crouching, sweeping the soil back with frantic, sharp jabs of the spade.

There was something ominously aggressive in the entire act. This was an enemy. He was straining to destroy it. With each shovelful, the enemy seemed to grow and was instantly matched by his anger and his strength. Now returning to the earth, with the enemy losing, he was sealing his victory with every ounce of strength he had.

I could hear him panting heavily. He was slowly exhausting himself. Then, suddenly, it was over. The ground was flat. In a final, angry gesture, he slammed the shovel shaft deep into the soil. He left it deeply embedded and upright. He turned and walked back into the cottage.

Behind me, in the cool darkness, Mrs Bezuidenhout still slept. As Kleinman passed me at the door, I could see he had been crying.

Briefcase
By Shirley Sampson

Every day, her much-admired Italian leather briefcase
accompanies her to work, incongruous on the proletarian bus
with holdalls, totes and lumpy shopping bags. Safe on her lap
its elegance belies its covert mission, like an old
aristocrat bent secretly on counter-revolution.

Inside her exquisitely-crafted nut-brown briefcase,
(fashioned from no less than seventeen different types of leather)
lies litter of her own existence: make-up bag, umbrella
diary, church keys, library books, a concert ticket stub –
the tissues of a middle-aged and solitary life.

But dark recesses of her co-conspiratorial briefcase
hide relics of an ill-timed love from half a life ago:
six letters and a photograph signed, 'Yours forever, Paul.'
This well-thumbed treasury of notes, her life's investment
waits impassively for dubious redemption.

So in the company of her trusted leather briefcase
she often takes the bus to libraries near and far, and similar
stores of documents and voters' rolls. She looks for signs
of him in dry-leaved, dusty registers, hoping to find
some kindling for fading embers one last time.

And she, resilient as her stalwart leather briefcase
will persevere. She'll not concede defeat till kindly time
invokes its alchemy, transforming all her barren
memories to fruitful Autumns – and her days, at last
to dreams as tender green again, as Spring.

Ring A Ring Of Roses, A Pocketful Of Posies...
By Rosie Mapplebeck

Lying in darkness unable to sleep
coughs wracking body like choking sobs

emotions too long held, bubbling
up to surface, witnessed by a night owl

>*"Don't expect anything from us"*

In the inky soothing dark beyond glass panes
rose leaves gleam, reflecting

street-light glow, waxen coats
twisting, tossing in untameable winds

>dancing in the smooth blackcurrant night

>*"You'll never be anything"*

echoes through unconscious mind
shaken out by hacks of hate from

generational frames of mutual-destruct
deep consuming us for too long

>*"Have you finished yet?"*

I spit, disgusted by the rank and bitter
poison, barbed and twined so deep, cast

out into the gentle all-embracing
tissue dance of wild and thickest night

Darren Unlearns Loneliness At The Old Country Inn
By Alistair Baptista

SAD DARREN
I'm lonely today barkeep, so I'll drink a few.
Because there is nothing else I can do.
I told her I loved her, I even said it with flowers.
I had to sit through the traffic for more than two hours.
And so many other things, that she doesn't even know.
But she loves another, and I was forced to let go.
And so here I am now, at my favourite haunt,
Living without the girl that I want.
Charlie, you've got such a wonderful smile,
And here I am now, the loneliest man for miles.

SMILING CHARLIE
Cheer up young Darren the day isn't done.
There's plenty of fish in the sea, she's not the only one.
The bachelor's loneliness is the married man's freedom.
Your demons will thrive for as long as you feed 'em.
You'll do better than her, just give yourself time.
Let go of your worries, have a glass of wine.
You've just dodged a bullet and you've still got game.
No two cherry pies ever taste the same.
You've still loads of time to score,
Don't bring your mood down son, we've heard it all before.

OLD BARKY
So you're lonely today, that's no big deal!
At least you don't have to beg borrow or steal,
To fix this problem we don't reinvent the wheel,
Sleep on it tonight, after a drink and a meal.
There's no real cause for us to console,
Fill up your glass, let the good times roll.
Forget about her, move on, have a drink,
Take my advice, do not overthink!
I'll advise your smiling friend to leave you alone,
You better make tracks Charlie, your wife's on the phone.

CHARLIE exits

OLD BARKY
If you're lonely today, you aren't alone.

Your search must go on, like a hideous poem.
Millions, or more have already been snubbed.
While unspoken words leave some feeling unloved.
Are you doomed to loneliness, can you crack the code?
Will you find a prince, or kiss another toad?
Will you find a keeper, will she always stay true?
I guess you'll just have to do what you have to do.
Life must go on, the wheel has to turn.
And loneliness is something that can be unlearned.
So take heart, gentle friend, you've made it this far.
And you've got plenty that others would wish for on stars.
Count all your blessings, laugh all you can,
And before you know it, you'll be a happy man.

Gone
By Gail Dendy

When I am gone, and you have given away
my clothes, you will see, one day, another

who reminds you of me. And she will have
my coat over her arm, and walk the way

I walk, and she will notice that you've stopped
and are talking to no one in particular, but by then

she will have crossed over to the other side
of the street. Both of us out of sight: she, and me,

but what surprises you most is how you come now
face to face, alone, with all the best that you can be.

Brother
By Keith Nunes

my brother, soul sick today,
maybe if you'd lived
we could have been friends
you could have saved me
from these distressing echoes,
that blood we share
running like a benevolent stream,
you and me and a breeze
delicate and comely,
this ache
would slip away
and leave us with a gentleness I rarely touch,
you and me brother with nothing to fear,
but the doubt
chills,
cripples,
and you've gone
can't replace what we didn't have,
my brother lingering
and me wishing I was you.

My Lover, Loneliness
By Megan Macleod

My lover loneliness
how I align to your fine embrace
sorrow surrounds us, just you and I

My lover loneliness
Tear stained cheeks are your gift to me
But I find no solace nor comfort in thee

My lover loneliness
It's just you and I
alone in the dark
Night after night

My love
My torture
My aching heart

Shall we part?

Anticipatory Nostalgia For Loneliness
By Abigail George

Once a table spoke
to me of a stark
goodnight. During the
day we rested our
frustrated hearts
over coffee. The cold
winter sun untrustworthy.
A god has painted a blue
shirt on the sky. I am
still in love with children.
With having children of my
own one day. This was my path
in becoming a woman.
I imagine him flying to
the moon. Playing golf.
On Sunday mornings.
In love with someone else.
Night swimming. He's with
with someone younger.
The lonely haunts me.
Midnight is a scar,

a panorama. You
are the present and past.
You are cold. You are heat.
You are just a boy. Eddies
of dust compared to me.
I am strewn with an ill
feeling of ordinariness.
I am like animals built for instinct.
Keep the animals safe.
They have dreams too.
For our limbs are restless
and much too long. Annoyed.
Frustrated by the sensitive,
the psychological.
Worshiped yet separated
by the glass ceilings of race,
gender, class, faith.
When the world was older,
hours colder, galaxies

less complex, traffic and people,
media less complicated.

Love is sport. Flight.
He is the one who would
understand why I call
myself a feminist these days.
He was lucky in love.
I was not so lucky.
There are movements
at the kitchen table.
The cat rises phoenix-like.
There are lonely weekdays.
I think of mountains standing
still under sunsets, clouds,
foliage green. The sky
slamming heat and dust
onto the beach, into rivers.
I think of faltering
pioneers. The fattening of potbellies.
I think of you madly.
I dream of you. The goal
was always love.
Of course it did not work

out in the end. The relationship
roaring into the ashen.
Roaring into the profound.
Even the landscape of loneliness
has its exotic borders.
Its boundaries.
There's a woodenness
to the tenderness
that I find at the beach.
I'm intoxified by the activities.
Most of all by the children.
I think of mountains
standing still when I think
of the cover of loneliness.
You, you Catapult most
of all inspire.
Am I tragic and lost after all this,
after all this time?
I am just misty-eyed
for the past. For you.

You're fleck. Fleck.

Depression
By Ashraf Booley

The earth dances
gyrating like a feverish wheel
that shakes the ground beneath my feet,
my feet that do not move to the beat.

The mirror talks back at me,
chanting:
you are not enough,
you are not enough,
you are not enough.

The world screams for attention.
I hear nothing but the come-hither sounds of solitude
reeling me in like the catch of the day.

The world shrieks with splendour,
extending a promising hand
but I unclasp from its grip
and drift towards eddies at the river's edge.

The Arrangement
By Karishma Krishna Kumar

She adjusted the necklace to sit in the crook of her collar bone,
The *duppatta* slipping uneasily off of her right shoulder.
The *bindi* looked crooked, so she bent closer to the mirror of her dresser and set it straight.
It caught the light above her and sparkled back.
The sparkle that ceased to translate itself into her eyes.
Her lipstick perfectly adorning her paper thin lips, her kohl lining her dark brown eyes.

"You look lovely", crooned her mother.
"He should like you. At least I hope he does.
You aren't getting younger. You used to be much prettier.
I really pray that he can ignore your height, or rather the lack of it.
Don't tell him you smoke alright? Don't tell him that you eat meat, okay?
And please cover the tattoos. It makes you look like an escaped convict."
All her flaws laid out on the table.
Flaws?

She adjusted her earrings one more time.
The tea had been painstakingly made, so were the dosas.
She whispered a silent prayer.
Please; please God, let him not reject me.
Thirtieth time's the charm? Thirtieth time lucky?
She hoped.

Balancing the goodies laden tray she gingerly sauntered into the room.
All eyes rested on her. Her steps hesitated.
She heard her mother animatedly discussing her.
"She wants to study more. I said how many more degrees do you want?
Which boy will marry you if you have so many degrees?
She applied.
I told her she can go if she gets rejected.
But, I really hope you don't reject her.
She is a good girl. She can cook very well, you know?
You should see the kitchen, it's spotless. All is her doing."

Her mother's voice sounded like a plea.

After twenty-nine boys had rejected her, her mother's faith had
begun to wane.

Her father sat silently at the edge of a sofa in the corner.
His hopes of her early marriage dashed numerous times over.
Why won't anyone just agree to marry her?

She looked up at the boy. He smiled.
She looked back down to the rug on top of the tiled floor.
"Sit down", the boy commanded her. So she did.

"Oh why don't you both go for a walk? Get to know each other?"
Her mother chimed;
Before she could lower herself into the chair she had been asked to
sit in.
The boy agreed.

She walked two steps behind him and listened;
While he talked of the large house, the large car,
And all the other benefits he was willing to offer to her.

Her mind notoriously unthankful, drifted to the man she had gifted
her heart to.
The man who didn't speak to her like he was doing her a favour.
But also the man who didn't want her.

She fixed her eyes back onto the boy and urged herself to focus.
"What is your dream?" the boy asked.
"To be a writer", she solemnly replied.
"Can you cook?" he probed.
"Yes", she volunteered.
"Do you want children?" he continued.
"Yes. Many." she countered.
"Okay. Sounds good."

He began walking back towards her house.
"I'll let my parents know what my decision is", he offered.

The jewellery set aside.
The *dosas* rubbery and cold.
She waited.
For the letter of acceptance.
Or that of rejection.

Bereft
By Rohini Sunderam

Your leaving would take the middle out of my life. To say that I would miss you is like beggars' alms, for they are a beggar's words. I would be desperately alone and the world would not know it. I would laugh as I always have: too heartily. But, I would not cry. To think of life without you would be like drinking tea from a saucer, too hot and then too cold. It would be like climbing Mount Everest and not finding ice and snow there, yet having lost a limb to frostbite. To think of every day, crystallising without you is emptiness so vast I cannot comprehend it, like light not comprehending darkness. The very aliveness of the world, the very death in me, a zombie; gyrating from one true pure function to another; that would be me without you.

The loneliness of the heart you have already known, but picture the strangeness of my soul without you.

Apart
By James Scalise

Apart. But parted not.
Our hearts, I pray, remain as one,
In touch through time and space.
Though sadly touching not.

If only time and space so favored love,
I would always be there,
it would always be now
and there would be
no reason for such rhyme.

In time so long and space so vast,
this love would have indulged
such yearnings only dreamed in dreams.

But when my hope seems all but lost,
I pray that time might change life's course.
And space – be just an ocean to be crossed.

For parted we will never be, even when apart,
Nor time, nor space, will ever dim,
the glow within this longing heart.

Cruise
By Sally Spedding

They said there'd be on-board activities,
lectures and shore excursions. Fishing
trips, hiking tours plus a turn on the Flam
Railway. So they said...
But loneliness has locked her bones, given
her tunnel vision, where all she sees is
a lone, damp deckchair, the funnel dropping
soot into her hair, on the best dress a size too big
in readiness for the daily smorgasbord of plenty;
pink, fatless ham and custard-coloured cheese
repellent under bright, bewitching lights.

They said there'd be a stop in Bergen for a three
course meal in convivial company, but she sits by
herself in the evening breeze, herring stink in
her nose. A mound of mussels on her plate, their
shells midnight blue with an oily cast, wrinkled
like her skin; She hasn't the heart to prise them
apart, break their defences, swallow whole their salty
lives...
They'd urged she try this seafood platter, but
when they find her, break her defences, there'll be
nothing save an anemone hiding in her ear.

That Special Little Boy
By Courtney Speedy

Six months in the womb
and taken by God too soon.
He was your beautiful son
and I know you were young
but I had no doubt in my mind
that you and him would be fine.
I remember the day it happened
like it was yesterday and I'm sorry
that I had no idea what to say.
I just wanted to take your pain away.
I had seen the hurt you felt on
my mother's face twice before and
it scared me how suddenly you
 ceased to exist and breathe.
Why did God let you leave?!
It's been almost a year
since you were conceived
but now you are bereaved.
There was a little heartbeat
that I couldn't wait to meet
and the sound of little feet
pitter padding up the hallway
and going into your bed
because he had a nightmare
and just wanted you there.
It's safe to say God only takes
the best ones away and
for that I feel anger each day.
I think you would have had
your mother's loud laugh
and straight up personality
because you would have
be stupid to bullshit
around with your mumma!
I'm not a believer in God but
I do believe that there is a
Heaven and your little boy
is watching over you day
and night making sure
that you are alright.
There will always be

those memories even
ten years from now
that will trigger tears but
that's fine because in order
to grieve we must accept
the fact that our loved ones
never really leave.
He's there in every
stranger's smile and
the breeze through
the trees as the
laughter of a child
echoes in your ears
and you know that
he is nearby and
his spirit did not die.
Please find peace
inside yourself knowing
that although you
and him may be
physically apart,
that special little
boy will always be in
your heart.

Coffee
By Simon Wong

A draught of cold air follows her as she squeezes in through the coffee shop door. For a moment, the smell of coffee becomes infused with the smell of the outdoors. A sound-bite of the external world is heard: a dog barks, a girl laughs, and a man shouts for a taxi, before the door snaps shut, and the coffee shop becomes lost again in its reverie. A few heads peer from behind laptops and books to catch a glimpse of this new apparition, but return to their original positions to minimise the lady's embarrassment as she "excuse-me's" her way over to the counter to buy a warming tea for one. The girl behind the counter mishears, and brings back a coffee. She looks down at it and murmurs a "thank you". No energy to explain herself.

She moves off to find an available table. She sits down with a sigh, glad to be out of the cold. The outside world is hidden behind a fog of bodily heat and winter cold. The smell of coffee wanes as she sits and stares out of the windows, wishing they wouldn't cloud up so much. Someone wipes a round shape into one of them to reveal the world outside; a cyclical place where time only existed in clocks, and she could lose herself, and think of any time but the present time...

The tinkling of a bell, the gentle touch of a breeze, and a short whoosh of air, wakes the old woman from her thoughts. She looks around in mild embarrassment, but no one has noticed her. She straightens her clothing and places her hands round the coffee cup, wishing it was tea. She shakes the cup, disturbing it, until the milky residue creates shapes like divination. By this time, the circle that had been made in the window has clouded up again, and she can see no further than the people crammed around her.

In front of her, she sees a man "excuse-me-ing" his way through the packed coffee shop. He looks up and smiles at her, making her red cheeks go redder. The wrinkled hands carrying the tray seem familiar, as does the wizened face. As the man approaches the table, the woman looks down at herself, hoping that there's nothing wrong with her appearance. She gets nervous, like a silly teenager, she thinks. She giggles at her own reaction, and looks up. The man with the tray is not there. A roar of laughter makes her turn round. He has his back to her, and places his tray down in front of a friend, who laughs at some private joke. She looks around in mild embarrassment, but no one has noticed her.

Someone gets up to leave their station, book in hand. The doorbell tinkles, and the world outside is heard: an engine grumbles, a car horn beeps, a pedestrian shouts. Then the door slams shut and the coffee shop becomes lost again in its reverie.

Losing Myself
By Dilraz AR Kunnummal

Losing my mind, losing myself...
A little each day...
Not knowing where this road leads
Dazed and confused...

Why is it becoming harder?
To keep my head high
Why is it so difficult?
To put on that smile...

I love my own company
Then why this lonely aura?
I love where life has taken me
Then why is a blue haze?

Why do I feel an insane need?
To let the dam burst...
How much more can I control?
Before the tears flow...

I look around and see happy faces
The opposite of my own
Its become a fight to survive
Amidst this lonesome crowd

So many noises around me...
Laughter love and joy
But all I hear is silence
Screaming in my head...

Maybe I need to take a step back...
Coil up like a fetus...
Maybe I should relax...
And start shutting down...

Breathe, I tell myself...
This moment will pass...
Close your eyes and hold on tight...
You'll wake up at last...

As I wait for my dinner to arrive

Sitting here all by myself
I wonder what the hell is going on
Am I losing my mind...
Am I losing me?

A Small Measure Of Peace
By Sameer Qamar

Seated in the dark,
Idle as a stone,
Lost in my thoughts,
Completely alone,
Misery not present,
A strange calm instead,
Besieged by peace,
Aloft in my head,
Cozy and comfy,
At one with the known,
Lost in my thoughts,
Completely alone.

The Old Fisherman And The Country
By Chandra Gurung

Dilbahadur Majhi
abrades his days to and fro the banks of the Narayani river.
He takes delight in being towards the village of waters
he wanders along the lanes of waters
and lives
a colorless, tasteless and formless life
just like water.

The old radio hung on the hut-pole
keeps on hissing-wheezing -
skyrocketed scarcity
topsy-turvy ill governance
news of messy management
and in another corner -
Dilbahadur keeps on catching in his perunge heart
those that have gone flying kites of desires in the sky of life
crossing the Narayani river -
chanting country on their lips
hugging the country all in their arms
oozing out the country from their eyes.

This country screams its agonies out
in every junction
walks bandhas and strikes in the streets
and kills the time of dark transition
Dilbahadur Majhi
keeps on stroking the canvas on the bank of Narayani river -
old eyes on guard of the house
youthful nights awaiting the incomplete honeymoon
young cheeks so restless to receive Papa's kiss.

This country goes away with so many
crossing its boarders
with so many it continues living in scarcity in its own yards
and with a porter pains enters into the city
carrying a huge burden of worries.
Dilbahadur Majhi
lives by the bank of the Narayani river
weaving a fishnet of so many thoughts—
crowds after crowds of scarcity-stricken lives
the blood and sweat that drain in the foreign lands

the song 'Here come the Gurkhas... '
that goes loud in the desolate battlefield
and the darkness of the red light area ...

Dilbahadur Majhi
lifting a globe of his wrinkled forehead
leans for a rest, breathing out his exhaustion.
If he could, he would turn them right back to their homes,
He would put up a hindrance for those
gone abroad crossing the deep Narayani river
adorning the country on the walls of their hearts
uplifting the country overhead
affixing the country in their hearts and minds.

Whereas
the country continues suffering in innumerable hearts
just like in Dilbahadur's bosom:
... plash ... splash
... plash ... splash.

*****

NOTES:
Dilbahadur Majhi - Typical Nepali name
Perunge - Catch basket used by fishermen to trap fish
Bandhas - Nepali word for closings
Narayani - Famous river in Nepal

I Am
By Gail Dendy

It was as if he'd never been, and that was
strange, since half my life had bound itself
along with his. We had travelled far

enough to know how red and angry the road
could be; had stood still long enough to hear

Blue Moon playing from all the neighbours' windows.
And I thought 'widow', not 'window', for although

he lay in bed beside me I was alone, and a garden
was growing at my feet. At my head there was

a monument, but the script on it was very small.
And whose name it bore I could not imagine, for in that

instance I began to believe in miracles. And then I awoke
and put on the new shoes he had bought for me.

Outside the rain was such that, the entire morning,
the whole town was wet, and where the poorer people lived,

their fires turned to smoke but, with the damp, such smoke failed
to rise. And yet hope was there among dust and ash

and this I gathered up. And then I brought it home.

Waiting Spaces
By David Hollywood

As you fly away the hours,
The miles, just time their day,
Absorbing all my patience powers,
I dream and wait away,
Between the spans of now and then,
Since ages, where you've gone,

Forbearance be, until you're here,
Stay all delays of when,
Those places late, despair to care,
Prolonged durations, Oh! Succumb,
The distance lingers, overcome,

My waiting spaces, minutes thrill,
The clock has ticked you back. Until!

Loneliness
By Lonita Nugrahayu

I am tracing all these words,
trying to find something,
that perhaps been missing throughout my life...
trying to find someone,
who perhaps lost on the way...
trying to find it, to find somebody
inside all these words that are merely my passion...
inside all these stars that have been leading me to my smiles' path...
inside all these beats of my heart...
Why still I am uneasy every time I pen my ink...
spilling ink has been the only thing I want to do,
why still I am feeling lost...
inside the peace of mind,
I still can't find my peace.
Is this loneliness?
is this how it feels...
chaos,
madness,
inside a passion that has been driven my soul to feel alive...
am I lonely?
Is it what loneliness about?
you feel like chocking yourself with your own passion...
What is it that has been missing in my life,
in me...
Is it you, sweetheart?
Do all these words would mean something if you would be here with me? by my side...
holding my hand while spilling the ink,
would all these words meant something?
If you are here, with me now,
would my passion towards the ink, mean everything?
But sweetheart,
since I have lost you,
I am finding you back through the words.
And now...
these words seem to have become the death sentence of
my loneliness since the day you left without looking
back, without turning back at me.

Alone
By Omar Ahmed

To stand aloof in the darkest night,
Needs a courage beyond the mind,
Where alone one is left to see,
What lives in the heart silently,
What need not rub against society,
That which nature delivered free,
Not to borrow concepts to substitute,
An authentic quest to experience truth,
Away and down into the inner world,
Unchartered lands left to be explored,
To face one's reality alone at noon,
And grace the night sky, a glowing moon,
Beams that spread love yet aren't concerned,
To whom, for what and which ends are earned.

Sharing The Journey
By Shirley Sampson

Against the unkind press of time
I searched my ample store
of words familiar and obscure
to pick and pack something to suit
the two of us in our
long expedition into grief
but words refused to settle and
as if I were a thief
they flapped around like anxious birds.

I quickly found I had no words
to smooth grief's jagged grain
but time and touch together made it plane.

Alone
By Farha A. Jaleel

Lost in the dark,
falling apart,
being sucked in a void.
Surrounded by walls,
emptiness fills my heart.

Stuck in a tower,
with thick walls -
so high.

Everything is a blur,
people passing by,
laughing with their loved ones.

Tears are falling down,
as I go by-
unnoticed.

Drowning deeper into the darkness,
There's no way out,
it's just me out there
I'm on my own...

The Bag Lady
By Maire Malone

Her shuffling gait
Moves her plastic home in twos
A square of faded carpet
Some stale chips and old bread
She settles down in her doorway
Of dark secrets

They say she had a child at seventeen
And that her family went wild with rage
No-one knew the father's name
In her dreams the Demon Shame looms large
Stifling an infant's cry

A charitable organization offered her a flat
Steel blue eyes lit up her weathered face
Lips unpuckered in a toothless grin
Sure I'm fine as I am
That's a bit of ax-minster carpet
I'll have ye know

She gave in in the end
When the winter was cold
But she'd sleep in an armchair
Not in a bed
Because she said
She'd miss hearing the chime

Awake for mass at six
To dine like a queen
A feast of bread and wine
She shuffles off into the morning

The Hole
By Claudia Hardt

What shall I do? I really don't know! Whenever I am in such a situation I immediately want to escape, want to make myself invisible, find the next little hole in the wall where I could sneak away like a mouse - sneak off through a dark hole into another world, to another place where whoever will be on the other side will see who I really am, how I really feel.

Where is the exit here, where is the hole? I desperately need to find my way out of this crowd, get away from all these people who look so important, talking about the newest gossip in town and acting like Mrs. and Mr. Perfect. Oh, I hate it! Why couldn't I just be a chameleon, changing my colour whenever the situation gets too uncomfortable and become transparent. This gentleman over there in the grey suit, he is staring at me since I have arrived, checking me out, moving his eyes up and down on me. I hope that he is not making an attempt to come over and talk to me. A talk that's the last thing on earth I am interested in. A talk, oh my goodness what shall I talk about? My palm starts to sweat. I am looking around. Where in Hell is this little hole which would give me a relief from my sufferings, once escaping through it? As much as I am looking around, there is no such hole, neither a big one, nor a small one. Sigh!

I move my focus from the wall back to the party scene. There, for a second I had the feeling the gentleman in the grey suit was about to make a move into my direction. Please, help! At least, all the other party-animals seem not to pay attention to me. Attention, that's the last last thing I need. Why should anyone pay attention to me? Does no one realize my emotional state? I have a look around again but I can't see the gentleman in the grey suit anymore, not in front of this contemporary and flamboyant orange painting where he was in a conversation with the eccentric host. I turn around. Oh gosh! My heart starts beating, my throat gets dry. He is coming over looking extremely self-confident, like someone who knows all the secrets in life, who is able to read my thoughts and certainly in between the lines. I am about to faint. Where on earth is this little hole I could escape to? Where is it? Why can't life just be easy?

I have a last quick look around, and? Oh yeah, here it is! Finally, I have found my little hole! Within the next second I am absorbed by pure darkness and pushed through a long tunnel with a bright bluish light in the end. What an incredible feeling! And what an amazing world awaits me on the other side, a world where I don't feel insecure, where I am me and where I can enjoy - without any constrains - what I like the most: Loneliness!

Salt
By Grace Ebbey

I'm small in my bathroom sink pouring spirits down my throat
I lick the back of my hand taste the salt on my tongue, it makes me think you're there
I shouldn't have let you convince me that people were anything more then people
That humans were anything more then human
You couldn't be responsible for what your heart does to your mind
What your hands do to your body
What your need does to them all.
I threatened to cut you out like a cancer
So you took your Chevrolet and the dog and the painting we made
And left
You told me loneliness is not a feeling
That it could be people
They burn the memories in and out of my mind
I wipe the sweat from my brow
Then watch my finger as it traces a name in the bathroom mirror
I see god in the mirror
I see god in the mirror drinking
And he's laughing - I'm laughing.
The memories. The memories.
They can't convince me, you were never here.

Out Of Africa And Into A Sea Of Discomfort
By Keith Nunes

an African man
but the noun seems misplaced
the name and the form of the man are misshapen components
awkwardly thrust into an engine that just won't run anymore
skins
accents
the seemingly perverse idea that you can be branded with a continent
even when you flee from it
but they'll tell you old fella that you don't belong here because they can hear you bend vowels around the BBQ
you're nothing but a novelty
and when the cut-throat markets cut their own throats and the dollar plunges into the Pacific and the government won't let any overseas skins in
they'll point
and they'll mention that continent again and wonder if you're behind their unflattering position in the OECD
and how the hell you could possibly be here in that skin
that doesn't look African
and isn't what?
English?

Lost
By Charmane MacGregor

I long for that familiar look of recognition in those pale blue eyes.
No shared memory, I reminisce imperfectly, alone.
I only have half the past for you were trusted with the other.
All at once a life's love lost and we are adrift in the continuous
present.

I have no reflection,
you see me only as I am now,
not the beauty I once was fixed in time by loving recall.

Finding Yourself Lost
By Cameron John Bryce

When you find yourself lost,
take them home, tuck them in,
and watch them drift off to sleep.
If they struggle then sing,
or read, or just comfort
them with words of love.
Often we run away
from our true selves because
we do nothing but throw hate,
beat them down, and bury them
under tawdry torment
that twists into grotesque
and dark acts of malice.
I've beaten myself so
badly before that I
found him laying with tubes
rigged to machines that just
barely kept him alive, and,
I tell you, it's taken
years for him to forgive
me, or even look me
in the eye. He would just
avoid my gaze from the
other side of the mirror.
Sometimes he would even
turn and run away in
to some fading idea;
some place where he could be
alone.
Alone without me.

Loneliness
By Vaijayantee Bhattacharya

Let us talk of loneliness
All of us together
How alone we always are
No matter how often we gather.
Let us talk of the only search
That has been on forever
For those two eyes and that sweet touch
Which no cruel time can weather.
Let us talk of the darkness then
That pierces our hearts like a dagger
And gets betrayed by a secret tear
On a rainy day or the other.
Loneliness is mine is yours
But we don't talk about it to each other
Who cares how lonely we cry in our hearts
Who's really got the time to bother?

Nobody
By Simon Atkin

I am nobody
What is carried
Are only movements
For you to see
Or feel as your needs
require

I am nobody
Just hollow shadows
From these bones
Through my skin
Rattle within me

I am nobody
This blood sticks to my bones

I am nobody
I stand aside as
I speak for all those words
Surley are not from me for I
don't know if I believe in me
as the me you see cannot be if
you see what I can see
of you

I am nobody
So leave me be and go to
change your world
Leave me with this rotting flesh
To suffer and die

Bloody Valentine
By Courtney Speedy

You once sung me
a bitter melody of
shattered glass
and bleeding thumbs
as we became undone.
You wrote your name
on the icy window
with blood fresh from
your wound and I had to
pretend like I wasn't bothered
by the pulsing veins and
racing nervousness I felt
as you signed it from your
Bloody Valentine

Open Window
By Alan Murphy

Nearby a pigeon
rehearses an aria,
the distant drone
of machinery
a faint rebuke.

One Night Stand
By Karishma Krishna Kumar

I slid the empty packet back under the pillow;
And walked out of the dreary room.
The rhythm of your breathing made me stop a while,
But, nothing could prevent me from taking the final step.

I heard the wind chimes clank away in a distance,
The familiar sounds and smells held me back.
Running my hand across the portrait,
I spent a tear in useless memory.

Stains of blood still remained in the cracks on the table,
The blade was long thrown out,
Left behind was the destruction it caused.
The swell in my hand itched.

Tired of picking up after you;
I let your leftover rubbish remain as it was.
The house seemed to eat at me,
Urgency hit me like cold, harsh wind.

Homeless but in lesser pain,
I'll light the past in vain.
Forming memories against what was,
I'll live again, maybe, for another cause.

Forgive me, in the light of a new day.
If you might, give the old rubbish away.
Stow away the unused passion, soon,
It will surely be a new morning, this June.

Sunshine, marmalades;
Pretty lights and torn curtains.
We'll hold each other again,
In some other lifetime.

Happiness
By Stu Armstrong

Happiness,
What is it?
It's talked of a lot
It's not something not many have truly got

To me it's the most import thing to achieve
If you lose it it's the worst thing to leave
Some of these people make me
Just want to heave

You can keep all you riches
And your beautiful bitches
My heart gets broken
It needs more stitches

It means fuck all, in the way of life
Happiness is all, No trouble or strife
All the money in the world doesn't make it be
Happiness is what I crave, everything to me

Some people are lucky
Happy with their lot
Happiness to me
It's not about what you got

It's the one thing I want
To have in my life
Can't seem to get it
Can't get a life

Even when things go my way
Just round the corner
There for me waiting
The devil makes me pay

Tragedy and sorrow
Are what I do well?
I am used it now
I stumbled and fell

I know now that it will elude

True feelings of happiness
Smiling and rude
That's not for me, can't get in the mood

This can be a terrible thing
Start to feel happy
In my head a bell does ring
To remind me I can't do it, can't do that thing

I want to be happy
More than anything there is
It seems so long
I shed more tears

Summer Days At The Mt. Eden
By Robert Hirschfield

The Wise potato chip bag has only one chip.
Alan Ladd steps into a river with one foot.
His horse sprints towards me,
or maybe towards the lady
in the bird's nest hat two rows down
by the fire exit
torturing a tootsie roll.
The empty black seats
cover their mouths with their hands
as if stifling yawns.
Ladd's sad eyes are looking past me
into the Bronx heat beyond the brass doors.
I am supposed to sit here
 until he shoots everyone who deserves to be shot.
The sky loses its way beneath his feet.

Is This What I Do?
By Lynda Tavakoli

On a corridor of fresh-painted magnolia
sunbeams stroke from Velux windows
onto freckled carpets, while a television
talks too loudly to itself in someone's room.

I find you sleeping, head sagged
as on a mis-hung coat hanger, hair,
just brushed, still full of war-time curls,
a legacy that did not pass itself to me.

I say your name, see the reluctant
wakening of your eyes, the disappointment
you had not slept your way to heaven.
You have told me this before.

Today we talk of blue dresses and funerals
and how you love my coat, and how
you love my coat, the colour redolent
of something already scudding out of view.

You ask me now if this is what you do,
just sit and wait, and wait and sit,
the resignation in your voice
the hardest thing for me to bear.

For in this room, that thief of time
has measured out its false remembrance in
the ticking of a clock, as the past becomes the present
and the present loiters somewhere in the past.

Love Reunited
By Christine Mcleod

Late one night my time had come,
To return home to my loved one.
Through my darkness came a beautiful light,
My heart relieved to have her in my sight

God called my name and reached out his hand,
I knew I have to leave this land.
But where I've gone words cant describe,
No fear or pain, just love and good vibes.

Don't cry for me or spend time being sad,
For to have shared your lives made me glad.
Remember the laughter and good times we shared,
Farewell my friends, until we meet again.

A Deadening Limbo Of Desuetude
By Rohini Sunderam

The empty blankness of my soul
Like a type on an artwork marked delete
Will it just lie there?
Gather stillness
Grow webs of desuetude
And fall into forgetfulness?

Forgive Me
By Lucy Reid

Forgive me I have been alone.
Unused to the face of conversations.
I am still figuring out how
thoughts get to speech,
or where to put my hands when I speak.

Forgive me I have been alone,
unpractised in body conventionalities.
This beating fist means I don't know how to start.
So, I don't or I do.

Forgive me I have been alone,
I do not know how to be myself.
Other than the rush and the need to say yes,
when I want to say no.

Forgive me I have been alone.

Where To Now
By David Hollywood

Where to now? all plans are lone,
Are up to what, whose dreams aren't told,
And then of sorrow, your ideals, own?
Just left to you, once plans are sold,
Instead of hopes through actions sown,
By promised changes, covenants' gone cold,
Well, on your way, you now unfold,
Crossed hearts untangled, twists of space,
Anaesthetise the times, not waste,
Above the ether, cloud a surfaced face,
There is no one who'd go the pace,
It was too long expecting haste.

Decay
By Ryan Joel

I am lost. Lost to the depths of this acrid heart. This dark void. This nothingness. It fills me. Every crevice of my being. Like water fills a cup. This darkness consumes me. And I find myself shifting. Drifting. Phasing.

My reality is morphing. The real and not so real become a distorted illusion in a warped mirror. The strangeness is inviting. I am curious. I like the cold. I like the numb. It feels like an awakening. I am deathly alive.

My words have no colour. My eyes are black without flicker. And yes. I am succumbing. To the darkness. My old friend. You welcome me home. My place of solace. Comfort.

My resolve is a rotten cadaver of promises. Lies and deceit. It reeks of contempt. But slowly. It begins to sweeten. I learn to appreciate the aroma. As it fills my lungs with its poisonous scent. It is growing on me. Becoming a part of me. And I like it.

And as in the darkness. I have no form. No substance. And as all unseen. Unfelt. Darkness. Where all that is not seen or felt. Can be discarded. Forgotten. It is here where I am at my most powerful. Hidden by the shadows. They hold me close. I am comforted by its lustre.

I am the darkness. Born from the belly of nothing. I am shapeless. I conform to nothing. And I cannot be controlled or harnessed. When warmth and fire recede. It is because I have swallowed them. I own them. And they cannot exist without me. Darkness is my servant. It will do my bidding.

When all is done and gone. I will be all that prevails. And I will consume all. That is my destiny. That is my purpose. For the light stains my eyes and burns my soul. In the dark I have comfort. Peace. Serenity. This is where you will find me. And though my soul flickers with faint light. Beware. It is a warning. You will be undone and privy to the same fate.

Love Comes
By James Scalise

Love comes at times on wings of flitting dove.
In rhythmic beat
of two hearts joined as one.

Love comes sometimes as blazing fire
to other hearts, alight
with passion, and desire.

For love will come in its own way,
So question not its sometimes sweet
Or sometimes lustful stay.

But savor every bit of bliss
Miss not its many fond delights
Enjoy it to the fullest while you may.

For as it comes, will also leave,
Will leave us so alone.
And in its wake a sea of grief and pain.

As drown in tears of doubt we ask:
Was that really love? And did it truly come?
And will it ever, ever come again?

The Failures Of Success
By Sameer Qamar

A young man with ambition,
And lofty dreams,
He's got it all made,
Or so it seems,
An imperious, large abode,
Bells and whistles, all the toys,
But on the inside, there's no peace,
Just misery, endless noise.

All alone in his world,
One he's made with much flare,
Amassing wealth, unchecked,
But not a soul around who cares,
Thankless and proud,
Obnoxious and loud,
Feet off the ground,
Dreams of flights in the clouds,
Like Icarus,
The narcissistic son,
Falling freely after flirting,
Far too closely with the sun.

Forsaking his loved ones,
The people who shaped him,
His folks and siblings,
The ones who always saved him,
Who always stood by him,
Though they had nothing to gain,
No favors or IOUs,
No debts to be repaid,
Unlike the machine,
That moulded him for its gain,
They stood by him steadfast,
Through all his joy and their pain.

Most of all his mother,
Who he'd driven insane,
Who'd wept all the time,
But never did complain,
Who'd wondered what happened,
Where did she err so wrong,

Nourished him with simplicity,
To be empathetic and strong,
Not cold and self centered,
Always chasing after wealth,
To be selfless and warm,
Always around to help,
"Time and tide wait for none,
But remember my dear son,
Use it well, build something good,
To make you proud when you're done".

But now it doesn't matter,
The billionaire beggar,
His expensive watch a reminder,
That the time has gone forever,
Priceless, his wealth a waste,
Folks walked out the door,
His siblings gone too,
Nobody lives there anymore.

Who wants to live in a house,
Where they feel all alone,
All anybody ever wants,
Is a cozy warm home,
The young man's awoken,
Sitting by his phone,
Waiting for the call, filled with hopeful dread,
The dread of being alone.

Pantoum Of Loneliness
By Simon Wong

Your loneliness goes unnoticed.
Your red lips turn purple, then blue.
As the nighttime fast approaches,
You ask how the cracked lines fell through.

Your red lips turn purple, then blue.
The pain in your brain is the truth.
You ask how the cracked lines fell through.
What happened to your playful youth?

The pain in your brain is the truth.
Time lied, and moved faster than planned.
What happened to your playful youth?
You stare down at old person's hands.

Time lied, and moved faster than planned.
As the nighttime fast approaches,
You stare down at old person's hands.
Your loneliness goes unnoticed.

Limewood
By Gail Dendy

I had taken a journey past a ring of lime trees,
which stuck in the memory, both the limes
and the journey, though where I was going

I could not imagine. This was one month
beyond my birthday. I could not have aged
much in that time, but I thought I was old

enough to distinguish the pain. The pain
of that journey, I mean, the one of separation.
I knew of the other journey too,

the one of Abandonment, but it was a place
so new and unrelated that I dare not
go there. The signposts were down and the gate

which led to a path was broken. There was
a field, though devoid of grass. At its centre
was the stump of a tree, and the remains

of an axe. I turned back to the scent
of the limes. The fruit themselves were hard
and green. Perhaps they were greedy for attention,

having nothing about them of interesting shape
or colour. It was hard to distinguish the limes
from the leaves. I thought of a place and a name:

Limewood. It was a place in my head, but
my heart was beating and the deafening noise
cancelled out thought, and touch, and smell. There were

only the bare prints of the journey of loss. And these
I wrote in my book to preserve what they meant,
and to save them from the limes and the scent of all else.

A Million Empty Words
By Zahra Zuhair

Ping. Ping. PiPing.
She picked up the phone and smiled.
'Nice dress?'
'Very pretty.'
'=P'
'xoxo'

Ping. Ping. Ping.
XDKisses sent you a video.
Ping.
Ping.
It was 10am and the weekend had just begun. It was too late for breakfast and too early for lunch. The curtains were still drawn and the light remained a stranger to her gloomy, well air-conditioned room. She could hear the washing happening in the kitchen and the pots coming out for the preparation of lunch. Soon, the various smells of the kitchen would make their presence evident throughout the house and her mother would enjoy it. It reminded her of the old days, back home, she said. In the country, up in the mountains, where trees grew in abundance and people laughed together around an oil lamp. Where the air was fresh and conversation was long and lively, where people looked into each other's eyes when they spoke and hugged each other when they were happy.
That was as foreign to her, as this was foreign to her mother.

PiPing. Ping. Ping.
Tomatoes sent you an image.
Tomatoes sent you an image.
Tomatoes sent you an audio message.

'OMG! She told me she never wants to speak to me again. All because of that image. She's crazy. As if no one has ever seen them together before and now she's suddenly afraid of what people will say? Please!'
She looked at the images. 'All they do is fight'. What else have I got?
'Skype party. 7pm – 12am. Bring your own drinks. Bring your own laptops. Be there!'
'By Yourself. Performance Art Exhibition.'
'Brunch?'
'Sure. Would love to.'
'Meet you in an hour?'

'Cool.'

Ping.
'You coming tonight?'
'For?'
'By Yourself'
'I don't know. I'd like to be social but I'd rather do it in bed today…. =P'
'I know what you mean.' 'I'm performing though.' 'Please come.'
'Yeah? What're you doing?'
'They give us a glass cubicle with almost nothing in it. We stay inside it for as long as we want to and do what we like. People can come and watch us.'
'Wouldn't they get bored?'
'Not really. They'd all have their phones with them. So, they can do something while observing us.'
'Hmm. I guess I could come.'
'Thanks'.

She thought it was a waste of time. Why would I watch people be by themselves? She got out of bed and headed to the bathroom. The water was warm on her skin and quickly turned cold when she was back in her room. After fifteen minutes of making a decision on what her attire should be, she was ready.

Ping.
'I'm here.'

She had a quick exchange of words with her mother, who was in the kitchen and she was out before the spices that had perfumed the house could cling to her beige cotton top and short, black, frizzy hair, still a little damp from her shower.

A quick exchange of greetings. Ping. Ping. Pippping.

Solitude
By Lonita Nugrahayu

Solitude,
has reminded me of you.
As solitude was our escape from everyone,
from everything.
And inside our bubble of escape,
we united.

Silence,
has reminded me of you.
As silence is your way now,
to escape from me,
from us.
You have built a bubble inside you
and keeping me outside...
wondering, screaming,
while you just stood inside there,
watching me in your silence.

Where am I supposed to go now,
solitude and silence can't escape me,
as being silenced in my solitude,
would only bring me to the bubble of emptiness.

And emptiness,
is the loneliness that creeps me from inside,
until I am dying from the life that should be lived in.

And dying,
is scarier than death itself.
Dying is more lonely than the loneliness we feel six feet under.

The Solitary Warriors
By Irwin Rego

I sit on the seashore, admiring the marvel of the oyster
A wonder of nature, radiating happiness unconditionally, to a world lost in its quest for vanity.
I ponder. It shoulders the discomfort of sand into its shell yet fashions a beautiful lustrous pearl.

I sit near the lake and gaze at the silent existence of the lotus.
A beauty transcending picturesque boundaries - giving pleasure to a world lost in its unsightliness stance
I ponder. It is unhindered by its muddy surroundings yet elicits serenity and magnificence in its appearance

I sit near the temple and hear the divine harmony of the flute
An instrument of bliss, unheralded - bequeathing absolute joy to a world lost in listening to its own voice
I ponder. It is cut, sawed, hammered yet brings about a heavenly melody - soothing the mind, heart and soul

Solitary Warriors, wonderful and beautiful instruments of our maker. Lessons to be learnt for us mortals - as we moan our worries, pain, problems, anxieties etc lest understanding its transience passage - planting trees of stress in our daily living fields.
Sticking out like a radiant kite, swaying against the ensuing winds of adversity - is really what makes the solitary self resilient, alive and promising!

Unconnected Senses Sought, Hopeless Depression
By David Hollywood

Unconnected senses sought,
All about. I feel distraught,
In now abandoned desperate need,
Of favour plus a place and creed,
Where depths for all my longings pine,
I'm wrenched so hard, that I am thine,

And as I struggle at a pace,
In this awful hollow place,
Introversions weary wait,
 Must not resist this spot, my fate,
Or tackle destiny, upset,
When time will through the truth beset,
Upon my ideals laboured toil,
And waste depressing hopes - my foil!

Connected
By Courtney Speedy

cars flashing
blinding lights
the city bites
especially this
late at night.
sad love songs
crooning on the
radio.
wind whipping
my hair around.
pale skin and
dirty smudges
on the windows.
cool words
murmured inside
a secret moment.
you are connected
to the stars in the
sky and the
lonely owl's cry.
streetlights slowly
switching off
for the night.
let's go home
you say
watching
steamy fog
contrast with
the snow.
keys coming
to life in the
ignition,
last diesel
infused smile.

Being Alone
By Toni Curran

Being alone and loneliness, as most know, are two totally different feelings. You can be extremely lonely surrounded by thousands of people. Being alone is sometimes a choice, which can be quite enjoyable. It gives you time to think and feel on a deeper level without distraction. Spending time with YOU, and finding out who YOU really are in such a busy and noisy world today is a special gift.

Most are scared to get to know who they really are, hence avoiding ever being alone at all. That's a shame really; as once you get over the hurdle of all the scary alone 'thoughts' you might initially go through. The other side of those thoughts and feelings is the real YOU. You can tap into and learn all about your thoughts and feelings. I have come to realise that by doing this, I am far gentler on myself now when I think, feel and experience different emotions. Almost like an acceptance process and allowing myself to feel the emotions and move through it, rather than trying to suppress them and in the end bottling them up and becoming an emotional time bomb.

My personal experience with spending a lot of time with myself, I feel, has helped prepare me for my future. Having the imaginary friends when I was little and always trying to find things to do to amuse myself when mum was busy. Mum and I always spent a lot of time together doing different things, going to different places like museums, parks and movies. When she was working, or at school holiday times, my skills of amusing myself would kick in. The gift or skill you develop being an only child.

I guess, as you get older, you become a little more used to alone moments. I remember a time in my 20s and early 30s that knowing one day I would be totally alone when my mum passes away absolutely horrified me. It was an incredible fear; I didn't know what I was going to do or how I would handle THAT DAY, when it arrived. However, in my mid 30s it dawned on me that 'I' was the one who had control over whether I stayed on this planet, and when it was time to go. No government or law enforcement were going to dictate to me how my end should be. Nor should I have to wait in some dank, morbid nursing home, rocking backwards and forwards waiting for Mother Nature to pull the plug on me. I guess it was my 'epiphany' moment, that once my mother has passed and I feel I have lived a good life and I'm still in reasonably good health and mind that I would be the one to 'pull the pin,' and make my silent exit.

Once coming to realise I was in control of my end, suddenly the fear I had all my life melted away and a feeling of calm replaced it. Most of society today shuns this notion, and I can understand that myself. I would definitely not take that road if there were things like pets or a loved one in my life that would suffer greatly from my actions. However, I would only be doing it if, at the end of my life, there would be NO ONE or no pets that relied on me sticking around. There will be a lot of people out there that won't agree with this decision, however, that's OK because as I've stated it's MY LIFE to do with what I please and it won't be affecting anyone else. So instead of wasting energy in judging my decisions, maybe use that energy to look inward and seek your own truth about who you are!

I am at peace with my life now, and I can't ask any more than that! Wishing you all find your own little island of peace too.

Online
By Sameer Qamar

Away with the loudmouths,
Be gone wretched selfie,
Blocked away the clickbait,
Avast ya scurvy hippie!
Someone stop this crazy circus,
So exciting it's a snore,
Holy moly my head hurts,
Promoting excess, more and more!
Every idiot's got an opinion,
An expert view on every topic,
Stretching out their 15 minutes,
Please, shush, stop it/

Everybody's a pundit of merit,
Some fake while some get it,
They've got "knowledge" so they'll spread it,
But 10 clicks later you'll forget it,
Be it Tumblr or on Reddit,
Bookmark or thread it,
Bathroom break's over your nitwit,
Exit browser or regret it.

Every site's just the same,
"Oh my God, it's sublime!
This'll change your life,
Click us this one time!"
They teach, preach and screech,
"Click here and socialize!
Ain't nothing waiting outside,
This is your new life!"

Well can't say that I blame ya,
Let's be honest, it does look sweet,
Fancy banners, spunky shading,
And the promise of being discrete,
Ah but they don't tell ya,
Is the thing that busts your sack,
Once you're on that domain,
You ain't never goin' back.

Shush, listen, do you hear that,

You don't? Good, neither do I,
That online paradise, that sanctuary,
It's a big shiny lie,
What, don't give me that look,
You knew it deep down inside,
Which fool thinks being lonely,
Represents a good social life?

That utopia you'd dreamt up,
That home away from home,
It's an asylum for deluded types,
Types much like your own.

Forgotten Me
By Simon Atkin

Wednesday morning
      the sky eased open
I remember you
      glistening, laughing myself
      amidst blood soaked
Thorns of glory
      I try to smile walking upon this concrete town
      but this world has forgotten me

I long to touch a lover's fair hair
These doors greet me with dreadful pain
I stroll slowly at my own pleasure
May I go now?

Grasping my fingers moist from my eyes
But this world has forgotten me

In Praise of Dambudzo Marechera's Loneliness
By Abigail George

Feeding the red beast
takes up space and time
just as much as a list.
A grocery list.
Too much space-time. Too much
time-space. The furious
red beast prefers
music to silence. The beast
knows when to forgive (Ambronese).
Knows how to live
with the loneliness.
Knows when to fish,
knows when to quit and call it a day.
Writers and poets have
built bridges over
troubled water all over Africa
before the advent
of America, foreclosure

and reality television.
There are many types
of good poets. Just as
many as there are bad
ones I imagine.
My sister and I were meant
for each other. Meant
to dance away from each
other out of arm's reach.
To thine own self be true.
Do unto others as you
would want them
to do unto you.
Words don't come easy.
I want to be happy
but there are I feel
so many challenges.
I must always be hiding away

from the thunder.
If a woman writes she
can have many adventures.

As many even as a man.
She has many advantages above
a man. She is intuitive
as well as being emotional.
Highly strung, anxious,
energised, restless,
frustrated by her bipolar efforts.
Out of loneliness comes
the divine. The birth
of the abstract of a poem,
Christmas, trees in autumn,
flight, figs, fun, jam.
Loneliness will let you
keep all of your neuroses and
The revolution hanging on.

In The Dark
By Farha A. Jaleel

I stand alone,
in this dark and dreary place.
The warmth has left me,
a chill sets in.

A deafening silence surrounds me,
the darkness-encompassing,
I find myself unable to breathe,
everything's falling apart.

I gaze upon a faraway light,
and make my way towards it.
But it gets farther away.

The wind blows fast,
everything's a blur.
I reach out again,
but stumble and fall instead.

I can feel the tears falling,
pain courses through my body.
I'm filled with despair,
it feels like a thousand knives piercing my heart.

There's no one to catch me,
-no one to hold me,
to let me know that it'll all be okay.

Someone who accepts me for me,
and wouldn't let go.
A reason to live on,
when nothing seems right.

I've been trapped in this maze
for far too long,
I can't seem to find my way out.

I'm all alone in the dark.

Gone
By J D Trejo-Maya

Open the window to see another type
of façade: look to the wall paintings
in Bonampak. There is more to see than
wants enclosed. You see the three forty –
five degrees in each corner. Artist can build
on minute intricacies as you see the window
in your eyes closing in... It is not yet all gone:
Tulum.

The World Turns Around Me
By Lynda Chouiten

The world is laughing,
Turning insolent eyes
Upon my weird, weird face;
The world is whispering
Words that painfully tease
My far-reaching ear.

The world is shocked
As I look back in anger
And throw a nervous "What?"
At its insidious gaze
And its hurriedly improvised
Mask of innocence.
I disappear...

Then I come back again
With stifled "whats" but dark, electric eyes.
The word is silent, the world is awed,
As my weird face breathes
And as I sign my victory
With a wan, lonely smile.

Strays
By Ian McKenzie

We are doing this in sixes,
We live off roots and grass
We scan the rubble horizon,
Waiting for hell to pass.
Me and the other five ghosts look up with half shut eyes looking for familiar as the house guts spill outside.
They don't mind as I pick first,
Someone else's teddy bear,
They do not grumble,
They do not mutter in dissent as I snatch a can of food,
Maybe they don't need it or simply cannot choose.
Then I pause and gather them round but I see unimpeded through them to the wreck - lined streets,
There is no congregating sound,
The shift and scrape of ten scuffed boots on broken glass or the sighs of bone-tired men with red-rimmed eyes needing rest,
Just the wind against me and the fractured open corners of the building,
And the thud-thud of my chest,
The truth is here in the tossed smashed plates and boiling brick dust,
I am alone and only remember them those that have passed.

Life Two
By Stu Armstrong

Life can be happy
Life can be sad
Ever felt to end it
Would make you Glad.

Day after day
Week after weak
Its wears you down
It makes you meek.

Minute after minute
Hour after hour
Its makes you want to hide,
Makes you want to cower.

Life can be happy,
Life can be sad,
Its really gets to you
It can make you go mad.

It's just keeps coming and coming
News that is sad
The kind that rocks you
The kind that makes you feel bad.

Its never lets up
Coming and coming
Can it get worse?
Am I under a curse?

Life can be happy,
Life can be sad,
When it's gone
I am sure you'll be sad.

Was I ever really that bad?

Grasping
By Heidi Al Khajah

Thin strands
They hold me
Together
I've been knitted
You see
By great seamstresses
But what if
One of those thin strands breaks
Will I fall out
Into oblivion?
I'm in utter despair
What will come of me?
Will I not be
Of this world anymore?

If it is so
Cast me into the sky
And let me be part of Orion
I think
I'd find pure happiness there

Dad
By Maire Malone

When my brother phoned to say you'd died
I was a child again running down the lane
For your ounce of condor or packet of gilettes
Knowing you'd say keep the sixpence change.

As I packed to come home for your funeral
I thought of you tying up bundles of papers
Under the stairs and the times I had come down
To the kitchen late at night and caught you
Kneeling by the sideboard quietly praying.

After your funeral, back at the house,
Mum saw your suit just hanging there
And cracked up.

My children talk of you a lot.
It hurts my throat when my son says
He remembers exploring the wart on your nose.

Kitchen Comforts
By Lynda Tavakoli

Resistance hugs the small kitchen
hiding secrets amongst
gloomy cupboard space,
post-war austerity brooding
on strained shelves.

Empty jars wheedle their
glass weight into the wood,
its protest stifled only
by the hum of a fridge –
a magic fridge procreating
eggs by the dozen
their longevity evidenced only
by an absence of feathers.

Plastic bags like artificial flower heads
scrunch in hidden corners
anticipating usefulness –
receptacles for ashes and potato skins,
swarf from box hedges,
odd bits of wool waiting for the charity shop.

An Easter cactus prospers on a sill
heedless of the pills that leave
their tell tale tips above the parched soil
where she drove them in.

This is the place she planned her day,
where through a kitchen window
the dulled reminders of her life
still resonated in the ordinary –
a rose she'd slipped,
blushing the oil tank in summer,
the remnants of a forgotten meal,
animal fodder on the lawn.

Nothing went to waste
not even the birdsong
wakening her at dawn
that somehow hummed upon her lips
for the remainder of the day.

My Uncle Don
By Keith Nunes

My uncle's tried to kill himself twice at Mount Maunganui. My dad says his brother has problems. I just say that he should turn to my dad because he fixes everything. But my dad says uncle Don can only fix himself. I see this like stitching up your own wound on a battlefield – isn't that what medics are for. So I say to dad, maybe uncle Don needs a medic, you know someone to talk him through it. Dad says that's all very well but our family doesn't have the money to pay for an expensive therapist. I say I don't know what a therapist is but someone who can talk to uncle about his problems would be good.

Uncle is a nice guy. He's nice to me and my sisters. He always has a smile and a pat on the back and he says to the girls that they look good and they love that. Anyway all the family really likes going out at the weekends to Katikati, or Waihi beach or Ohopi for a swim and a look at the art gallery. Uncle really likes the art by the artist Talulah Belle – he says it shines brightly.

I hope uncle doesn't die soon. He's too young. He had a woman friend he was shagging, said my dad. Whatever that means! So uncle was a journalist with newspapers and he had a bad time and dad says it was a breakdown – something about nerves. Then he was laid off and spent years doing jobs that were less than savoury, says mum. Soon uncle tried getting back to what he knew best – writing something. That turned out well but there was no money in it so he got depressed.

Soon uncle lost his shag and was living in his car down at Pilot Bay where he went to the toilet in the local loos. He said that was okay because no-one bothered him and he didn't have to answer to a woman – whatever that meant.

Dad said uncle could stay with us but I'd have to sleep on the couch. I said to dad that that would be okay as long as uncle didn't shag anyone in my bed. Dad said that would be okay. So now we have uncle in the house and away from the shady loos down at Pilot Bay and he seems happy to have breakfast with us kids as mum tells us to hurry up because we're late for school.

Uncle walks us down to the school and at 3pm he's there to pick us up. It's really cool to have uncle with us and I hope he stays with us and doesn't try to shoot himself or anything stupid like that. Maybe one day when I'm older uncle can live with me and he can shag his missus on his own bed. That would okay with me.

Alone In My Head
By Megan MacLeod

Alone in my head
As I sit and wonder
How did I get to this age
With the years asunder

Days filled with people
Many things to do
Yet crowds don't hide
The loneliness inside

Alone in my head
I contemplate
For my next move
To bring me peace

I Sat On Your Lap
By Courtney Speedy

I sat on your lap
last Friday night
and I said darling
are you alright?
Are you depressed?
Cause you're drinking
a bit too much
for a hot mess.
You looked deep
into my eyes and
I wanted you to
be honest with me,
tell me about your
mother and how
she's let you
down and how you
end up drunk on
the concrete ground.
Let me kiss your
lips just like another
girl did last night
and I'll tell you I
like it when you bite.
You say you don't
even think about
walking into a fight
and I can see there
is something behind
those eyes that have
seen something I
don't want to know.
You have a strange
name with an even
odder way of living
but who am I to judge?
You say your name
has been through the
mud and you want
to get out of this town
because it's just
dragging you down.

Yet I screamed at you
when you told me
about the bottles
in the back of the car
and how the girls
watch from afar.
You got angry and
shook the steering
wheel and I had to
shake my head,
was this even real?
You tried to touch
my shoulder and I
shook your hand off
because you had
said I wasn't just
another girl but
I'm looking at the
way you hold
me so surely,
so securely that
I know this is a
well rehearsed role
and the drinking
is beginning to
take its bitter toll.

Back
By Shirley Sampson

In time, you went back
to where you were once loved –
that small room by the sea.

Did you cry, I wonder,
or were the memories
welcomed like old friends
or comfortable shoes?

Now you're opening doors
in hollow rooms
disturbing sunlit dust
with your salty breath.

The voiceless, unfamiliar
silence weighs you down.
The gun, too, lies heavy in your hand.

Cocaine
By Courtney Speedy

you're wearing
bright red lipstick
and a little black
dress but you
are a mess and you
can't even give the
taxi the right address.
You smell of cinnamon
and sugar mixed with
marijuana and when
you laugh I can see
the fillings in the
back of your mouth
and I resist the urge
to touch your cheek
and feel the curves
of your body beneath
your clothes.
I can taste smoke
at the back of
your throat
and I remember the
way you once wrote.
I think maybe
I'll love you
until this cocaine
has left my veins.
What was your name again?

Why?
By Stu Armstrong

Why do you do it?
Why is it so?
I never wanted to let you go.

Why do you do it?
What is the reason that you hate me so?
After all you let me go.

You never get better
You never are true
What the fuck even happened to you?

You're out to hurt me
To teach me a lesson
Coming down on me like I am under compression.

You make me head want to explode
I only ever tried to help,
To carry your load.

How did things get this way
A life of hurt, sadness and dismay
That's how it is, no matter what you say.

You forget about how I picked you from the gutter
Did you hear my complain
Curse or mutter.

I put you where you are in life
When my insides dies
When I made you my wife.

I did everything
That could be done
In return I am under a gun.

You push and you push
You lie and cheat
You won't be happy till I am at your feet.

You are an expect at being vindictive

You want to take it all
Am I heading for a call?

I always gave you what was you wanted, I was more than fair
All you left me was debt
And very grey hair.

You're making me ill
But I know you don't care
A very sore head has this bear.

You want to just take
Not work for your life
No change there, you love your strife.

Just pay what's yours
For what you own
I am not your bank, you get no loan.

It's not to just me
You damage the kids
One of these days we will flip our lids.

Whatever I do
There's a sneer and a cough
Listen to me, why don't you fuck off!

The Deserted Beach
By Gail Dendy

I fitted my feet into footprints
hopelessly too small,
walked half-a-dozen paces
with these odd, truncated steps
then turned around once more
to find I'd aged before my time.

What to do? Walking backwards
was no solution. Waiting
for the rising tide to lift each footprint
off its sandy base would be
merely giving in. I turned, and left.

Next day, and the next day after that,
the miniature footprints
were back, criss-crossing the beach
then looping round in spirals
before ducking up the slope
across the kikuyu grass and beyond.

But by now I had the knack,
fitting my feet into each little cup-cake print
and shortening my stride

so that these little feet
now suit me admirably
and fairly march me to our door
of thirty years before

where I hear my father saying
(that day he left for good)
not to worry, he'll be back by winter,
and then I must wear my prettiest dress,
the one that looks like wind in the blown kikuyu grass
that time the gate was left unlocked
and swung wide open for the entire day.

Solitary Confinement
By Nilanjana Bose

I'd like to tell you that walls don't close in,
that domes of bones don't collapse or implode.
That things are fine, the clouds high and thin,
the usual paired headlights speckle the road.
The colours of loneliness are strong, piquant,
that their bright acid pigments do not corrode.
I would like to tell you that, but I can't.
Something in that analysis seems flawed.

We come and go alone, and it's good to pretend
there's provision of company in between
a lonely start and an even lonelier end,
love and laughter churned at whim into the scene.
It's good to think that someone will hold your hand
and friendship and love will remain throughout, pristine.
I'd like to tell you that, but don't understand
which words would fit exactly what I mean.

Then there's the principle that love liberates one
from the need to have it measured and returned.
That nothing of love is ever lost or won
on its being either accepted or spurned.
That it's easy enough not to miss attention,
and a response to each loveless day can be learned.
I would like to tell you that, and be done,
but somehow the phrases just won't be turned.

A misplaced faith that something will see you through
each loneliness will find an equal patience
to outlast every solitude; make do
with your own voice and an asphyxiating silence.
In all music, and from every point of view
the same platitude's repeated with confidence.
I'd like to tell you different, but it's not true
and my lines can't quite match up to the evidence.

It has been a long time since the walls closed
and domes and bones fell to ruins, remote
years, decades since the secret was disclosed,
left alone to echo its one, lonely note.
I would like to tell you what you supposed

was right, not some panicked, made-up anecdote.
I'd like to tell you that, but nothing's composed
and I can't find the cheery poems I once wrote.

Hollow As A Fallen Echo
By Irwin Rego

Promises, love and assurances just words empty and hollow like a fallen echo.
No one in this world belongs to anyone, these relationships are momentary – a fact hard to swallow.

Life's journey continues with close associations bringing transient elation.
The Irony of life where Kin and Friends are no guarantee of being there for you at the relationship station.

We continue living in lies, behind the beautiful façade of words – putting on false shows.
Revering holy creeds but forgetting our neighbour's anguish and blows.

The true essence of religion forgotten, interpreting it to our own whim and taste.
So full of ourselves, even the messiah today would have to search for grounds to save us– life lived in such haste.

Egos and Envy continue to reign supreme where we fly so high on the wings of vanity, losing sight of the meaningful connect and trust.
Like green leaves that wither to the ground, we seldom realize that we too one day will go down to dust.

People will be selfish and insincere, happy with you in your good times and break your heart in bad, at times with utter disdain.
They do it regularly to the almighty – to the absolute, so who are you oh mortal man to complain!

Promises, love and assurances – just words empty and hollow like a fallen echo.
No one belongs to anyone these relationships are momentary, a fact hard to swallow.

Death, Love, Hate, Blood
By Stu Armstrong

Death, the end, final
Your pain will leave you
With me you leave the pain
I will never think of you good again

I am lost, I'm deaf I'm blind
You may think now I am not the nasty kind
You're hurting me once more
Yet I can't even knock at your door

All I ever wanted was for you to rate me
Instead all you do is hate me
You're supposed to be my dad
But all my life you've made me sad

You think you're all the big men
But you will never feel love again
Sitting here hurting and thinking
Through my tears I am blinking

Remember you were the one that ran away
You were the one that ceased that day
I saw you that morning and I was a child
What I saw I wished to god I was blind

That was the day that I found out what you are
A small child watching and crying in a car
I will never forget just what I saw
You couldn't even come over and open the door

Then I got left with an embarrassment to you
Just another one at the back of the queue
Messages from her got relayed to me
That was the fucking bitch that betrayed me

That was the so called beloved sister
Bitch is as poisonous as puss in a blister
I hope what you have all done you think you are clever
Because I tell you this, me, none of you will have ever

I am sitting thinking at work

An about me you don't even twerk
I am only your son after all
But you didn't need to make me so small
You may think I am strange
But to cope I write
For you to get by
You just don't give a shite and die

How you can hate me for a child
Young enough to hit meek and mild
I try as I might to look for the good
But I just don't see the trees from the wood

Maybe if my name was Vodka
I would make you proud
But at the end of the day
You don't want me around

I tried my very best
But all I was, was a pest
You hurt me and hurt me and hurt me again
Even since before you left me
Before I was ten

I can't believe in death you're so hateful
For god's sake dad am I so distasteful?
Why the fuck are you doing this to me?
I guess I was never who you wanted me to be

Death, Love, Hate, Blood
Whatever I try I am still no good
At least I know your family tree
Every last one of them is dead to me!

Sightless Loneliness
By David Hollywood

When shadows gain their view,
In mine's, through blackened faces,
Looking for the order, sought
In depths, far down below, our thoughts... all fail,
Into abyss where, and from now on, we're few.

In pits we fall to know,
And lonely voids of common greetings, echo in a dream,
Of loved ones images, once we knew,
Now covered by the hue,
Of heart burnt losses made to show,
There's something in a seam,
Just hemmed together in a light,
Of darkened ceilings sealed.

And caverns of our feelings caught,
The shadings glimpse,
A reel,
Pull blindly, at what shows the sight,
Of lurching moods and lowered bright,
Nor sound, within the night.

Of loneliness, heard in our gasps,
And all our feelings rasp.

Fatal Attraction
By Ryan Joel

His hands quivered. Wavering. Unsteady. He swallowed hard as he slowly raised the loaded pistol. It felt like it weighed a ton. And then he felt the cold steel pressed against the roof of his mouth. He closed his eyes. Body trembling. Tears streaming down his face. Salty beads of sadness running down his hands. Embracing the cold steel of his adjudicator.

He whimpered. And committed himself. This was it... He would finally be free...

Free from the pain. Free from the hurt. Free from being different. Free from being alone. Free from being unloved. Free from feeling worthless. Free from this twisted, cold and harsh reality. And for him. Life was hell. And living was torture.

He loved her. Loved her so much that every fibre in his being cried out her name. Only. He didn't know who she was. Or where she was. He didn't know her at all. Only the colour of her soul. How it shone. How it radiated. How it touched everything. The fire within her sang fiercely. It sang to him. Only He could hear the song. It was vibrant. Chaotic. Yet so soothing.

When she smiled. It filled him with purpose. He didn't know why. He just knew how it made him feel. Her laughter resonated deep within him. And her presence danced across every fibre in his body. Chemical. Intoxicating. Electric. It was surreal. Yes. Surreal.

And when his thoughts left him. The world was grey once again. Colourless. Lifeless. Without pertinent meaning. The difference was. He had seen her. Many times before.
On the bus. Buying coffee. Reading a book on a bench in the park. Always the same. Always a million light years away. Unfathomable. Unreachable. Mystic and forbidden.

He swallowed harder. Almost choking on the barrel of the gun firmly pressed to his palate. A stifled cry. Shaky hands. One million light years of thought flooding his mind in an instant. And all worth nothing.

He had never stood a chance. Not being who he was. As much as he admired the beauty in her fire. It would consume him. And leave him burnt. Spent and useless. Her fire was not without reason. Fuelled by ages of pain, anger, hurt. Any who dared brave it would feel it's wrath.

And for him. That was worse than death itself. Death was singular. Pain was plural. And that made complete sense. And of course. The logical choice was made. Maybe in his death. He would finally meet her. Their souls would embrace in an eternal dance in the cosmos. And if it were just a dream. He would dream it a thousand lifetimes over. He would finally know happiness. Feel love. Give love.

And this fatal attraction would be infinite. Complete. Catastrophic. It would be like the birth of a new star.

Beyond Strength
By Heidi Al Khajah

I'm tired
No
I'm exhausted
I've spent every last part of me
I want to grip hold
Take your innards and breathe
I'm beckoning into the abyss
And as I fall
I think
This is something different
Caparative
Yes that was purposely done
I'm. Captive.
I want out
I am running now in my mind
I'm running free
And I wish for it
I wish for that warrior
To take over

I've been running in my mind
In my mind I've been running
Too long
Too damn long
My warrior takes flight
As it is released from me

What Could Be More Romantic
By James Scalise

What could be more romantic than a Grand Tour of Italy? In springtime - in this Mediterranean paradise?

What could be more romantic than the sprinkling, tinkling, cascading waters of the Fontana di Trevi? The world's most magnificent fountain, splashing from overpowering travertine statues of the gods of Oceanus, Abundance, Fertility and Joy, refreshing this worldwide convergence of lovers and friends below, on an especially joyous Italian celebration, Easter evening.

Couples arm-in-arm, guitarists serenading their friends – or everyone. Spontaneous outbursts of joyful song throughout this open shrine of love. Coins tossed in merry tradition in appeal to the gods for health and love. Happiness everywhere.

Or so it should be.

What could be more romantic than a long ride up, down, and through the hills and valleys of Tuscany, panoramic views from oversize bus windows framing a world of never ending paintings-to-be? Every window focused on some other unique fleeting scene in this all too real painter's surreal landscape. A flow of form and color, of vineyards and arbors, tall Tuscany Cypress and plump olive trees scattered all about. Arched and columned white plaster villas with reddish tile roofs, splashed with flowers in every color of an artist's palette: Lemon Yellows, Orange Reds, Olive Greens, Grape Purples and uncounted others. A chorus of romantic artistry everywhere.

Or so it should be.

What could be more romantic than the ambiance l'amore of a candlelit dinner in an intimate Venetian café on the Piazza San Marco, overlooking the Grand Canal? On the platter: a traditional local specialty of fresh marinated codfish Baccala Montecato and Polenta. Serenaded by a roaming ensemble of out-of-season opera stars, appearing magically at tableside. Reminders of Casanova. Romance in the air.

Or so it should be.

What more romantic than the scene outside the café window, of gondoliers rhythmically stroking their long oars on a quiet glide through the canal. Serenades softly blending across the waters as the boats meander in no particular hurry. Heads of lovers softly resting on shoulders, silhouettes from bridges probably smiling down, lights from the windows of houses lining the canals playfully dancing across the black waters. What more romantic?

Or so it should be.

So romantic. So romantic that it was overpowering. So romantic that it brought tears, tears of sadness, not of joy, to what should have been the happiest of settings.

Surrounded by joy I was miserably alone - there was one thing missing in this wonderland of love:

A special someone to share it all with.

The loneliest I have ever felt.

Alone
By Karishma Krishna Kumar

She sat at her window and stared,
Stared out at the green grass;
The beautiful hibiscus bush,
The flowers were all grouped together.
All were in a bunch.
Except one, it stood solitary;
Alone

A lonely little sparrow perched itself on the bush,
Gaping at the nature around it,
Looking out for company;
Any company, but,
Among the flowers, the grass and the sun, it stood;
Alone

Then came dusk and the sun began to hide away,
Plunging the garden into darkness,
She was scared of the night,
Another page is over.
The page will be turned and a new page will begin,
This page will be lost,
This day will be lost,
Another chapter will close, and,
Another memory of loneliness will be created.
Alone.

****

Its bedtime once again, and,
Crying under the covers, she whispers;
"Please mommy, don't turn off the lights",
"Please, not tonight"
She is scared to fall asleep.
Alone

Acres I Imagine
By Cameron John Bryce

To nowhere I go in the nothing I feel,
Spinning like an old coin or a wayward wheel.
I tumble as I twist, throwing myself on
through the falling mist of the new red dawn.
Battered as I bounce, I trip on with zeal;
Spiralling, Spiralling, Spiralling on,
till I'm spiralled from anything I thought to be real.
Till concrete crumbles and the green grass is gone.

Here, I stand, in those bizarre acres of mine.
Where geometry fails in the plans I design.
Where math melts like memories of my boyhood,
and the laws of motion cripple to be understood.
Come falling upwards, plummeting to the sunshine.
We'll swing and we'll sway on the old wise wood
of trees that hang from the skies like a shrine
to nature in reverse, and truths in falsehood.

Under The Bed Wallowing
By Keith Nunes

the room fills with her children and their attachments
all talking at once about how incompetent and rude
the others are

somehow, everyone has a better relationship than their siblings
and so much better than their mother's
who is married to an indolent buffoon

I take it in good humour, then, after I do the dishes, I slip away
to hide under the bed like I did when they were younger and all home
as I lie there, feeling safe, I relieve myself.

Missing You
By Rohini Sunderam

The stars made pinpricks in the dark curtain of night
The moon would not be rising
The night wasn't for moonlight.

The halo around the streetlamp whirled
Spinning in a mad rainbow turmoil
The light of a firefly stammered along
In a code that no one can foil

I sat in the darkness waiting for dawn
Which was still so far away
A clock struck eleven
While I counted seven
Whole hours for day.

Then I shut my eyes and tried to sleep
But sleep would not come
For you had left me alone.

Away
By Shirley Sampson

...for Richard

We'd meet occasionally when we had to –
when our attendance was required at some
big family event. We'd take our time –
no longer any need to rush to seek
each other out, strain ears for voices,
look for gaps in crowds to glimpse through.

After a while you'd just be there. You'd say
Hello. Ask how things were. There'd be the slightest
brush of finger tips on shoulders –
a swift fly-past of lips on cheeks; a little smile
an echo almost imperceptible
from those distant shared life-years away.

And yet, forty years on, I wrote a lot
about you, wondered what you'd think –
was sure you'd read my words some day
and we'd discuss our recollections, laugh
at all our funny stories one last time –
but now I'm told, you're gone; you've left. You'll not.

Suddenly the world has aged, gone grey.
Outside, familiar streets come to the door
like prying neighbours; lamp-posts leer like drunks
through windows at a horde of worthless memories –
which, like unspent coins of disused currency
this old curator will now lock away.

Addiction
By Courtney Speedy

Her parents warned her
about drugs on the street
but she didn't think she
would find the worst of
all in a heartbeat.
His mouth is cigarette
smoke and his limbs
outstretched are syringes
with a syrupy liquid in them.
His skin is mottled with
code words for the black
butterfly which puts all
his ex lovers in the sky.
Does she want to die?
Because that's how
it's looking today with
his devilish ways.
His words are marijuana
leaves and when she's
gone all her loved ones
will grieve.
He's got her caught up
tight in his claws
and he's using all of
her flaws against her
so when she's feeling
empty and sad she
does a line and pretends
that all is just fine.
Oh so addictive all for
a temporary rush but
what she felt for him
was more than a crush.
But all he sees when he
looks at her with his cold
hard stare is the pretty
blonde hair and the smile
that's got everybody except
him caught up in her happy
little world but it's all coming
crossing down with a lashing

of marijuana in the morning
and meth at midnight.
She's beginning to look
a bit of a fright with her
hair growing all out all
straggly and black bags
under her eyes from where
happiness once lay but
now the drugs are asking
for their bit of the pay.

A Lonely Heart
By Rosie Mapplebeck

Is there anybody out there
who speaks the same language as me?
with the same tastes in clothing or
variation of small degree?

So many seasons I've lived here
always hoping I'd find The One
while sounds intrude of trees falling
men clearing lands to farm upon

Lonely days waiting for a love
in my sparse corner of terrain
with no-one there to whichaka
just lowing cows, pattering rain

With Carraiba gone there's nowhere
left to rear my family in
even if I found a blue girl
where could our nesting time begin?

*

Mr Collector you come here
telling me now the times have changed
investment in where I come from
protecting lands where I once ranged

You say there's mates waiting for me
no cage shall ever feel my claw
I'm the last wild-living parrot
of the strain called Spix's Macaw.

Seven Minutes
By Sara Spivey

I'm now underground too, but mine is the Westbound platform of the district line. I am the sole occupant of this tubular shaped concourse. Written in amber above my head, the timetable shows the next tube will be arriving in seven minutes.

Seven minutes is long enough to spill out my tragedy, my agony of a sibling lost – regrets of what was not said. Seven minutes to tell you we were best friends, shared wardrobes, arguments and ideals. I find it inexplicable, she arrived after me but left before me.

The fluorescent lights sporadically flicker at the far end and are a stark contrast to the sooty black cut out hole running through the depths of London. A faint burnt rubber smell flickers across my nose and a gritty haze can just be made out at the gaping mouth of the tunnel. An eerie subterranean silence is offered me, the only voyeur to this unusual moment in time. However, not for long...

I tilt my head marginally in the direction of the sound of my intruder. From the corner of my left eye I spot a stout looking middle-aged man in an expensive navy blue suit and remarkably shiny black leather shoes. He's engrossed in a heated stop-start conversation on his mobile. I notice a couple of beads of sweat along his top lip as he rumbles right past me... close enough to touch.

Within the space of another three and a half minutes the platform is alive. A swarming mass of bodies and the commotion of noise duplicated with the acoustics underground. So many potential listeners, shoulders to cry on, but who? Perhaps the children chattering excitedly amongst their parents legs, or maybe the two young women giggling and checking lipstick. Even the elderly gentleman carrying his chequered shopping bag or at a pinch the scruffy musician with long hair wearing a brown waistcoat.

My reverie was momentarily interrupted by a metallic clanging way down the tracks. Two faint lights, a subtle warmth and the train whistled in with a breeze. The next moment or so was a cacophony of activity, people bustling, grabbing their belongings and ensuring a place. The doors closed, I was left watching an animated mime behind glass and then they disappeared into the distance, further underground.

Still nothing said. I was offered a chance of seven minutes to share with countless souls inches from me. Had anyone even really seen me I briefly mused? Now I'm back where I started, sole passenger heading Westbound, next train in four minutes. Anyone care to listen?

Loneliness
By Madhavi Dwivedi

It's not when you are by yourself
it's not when those viral voices go silent
it's not when you turn around
and the crowd is gone.

Loneliness is born
when bonds are broken
when connections between hearts crash
when souls are stolen
when that one melting voice goes missing
when your home is no longer
your fledglings' nest
when family shifts to cyber spaces
when communication is confined to "likes"
when your heart yearns but
has to wait for some permission
when the thousand faces around you
are distempered with those dead smiles
that your heart does not recognize.

Loneliness comes of age
When hopes hibernate...

Puppy Pees On The Lawn
By Maren Bodenstein

Ma says I must wait out here for the furniture van. They're two days late because it's far from where we used to live look I'm making pictures on the pavers you must break the leaves at the base and squeeze out the jelly it looks a bit like snot and then you can draw squiggles and faces like this and then you see it goes away because the pavers are hot and one day people are going to come and say we've never seen such beautiful vanish art and they're going to clap and oh there's the van see the wool from our carpet is coming out the back flying like hair like a flag ma is going to be furious the doors are flapping and all our things are inside and it's been so long since we saw our stuff from the old house because ma and pa went away and I was in grade one and I was in boarding school and I peed in the bed and they put the mattress out on the lawn in front of the hostel where all the boys walked when they went to eat and everybody was laughing and saying who peed in her bed last night but it wasn't me all the time Olga and Lynette's ma died so they also had to go to boarding school and some mornings all three our mattresses were lying on the lawn together and no one could tell who it was who'd peed in their bed. The men from the van are stretching their legs see they've brought a fluffy puppy they must've forgotten our old dog at the house ma shouts at them didn't you see the wool sticking out at the back it's for the family carpet we're making and they laugh at her in a friendly sort of way and start to unpack and puppy follows me around and all our things look so old come see puppy I can draw on the pavers with plants puppy pees on the lawn don't let that dog lick your face ma shouts you'll get worms.

A Direct Hit
By Alan Murphy

Some ordinary morning
Deft hands of hope
Offer a rare chink of light.

Eight minute miracle,
Quotidian,
Bullseye, the smirk of the sun.

The Truth He Tried To Tell Me
By Keith Nunes

a fine looking man with long salt and pepper hair sat down beside me in the bus running into town. we exchanged limp smiles. he looked unsettled, arranging himself like a modern dance student doing his practical exam. I had the urge to say "everything's okay".

he wasn't carrying anything. he was dressed like a seventies band manager and had several earrings. as we lurched into the first stop he turned slightly toward me and said: "I've always been sad. It's like spending your life at a funeral and you're trying to be the strong one."

he pinched me gently on the leg and left. in the hollow of the seat was a puddle.

Sharp!
By Abigail George

There is a ghost
nation that appears
after the swallowing
of aspirin.
The gasping
of mouthfuls
of dark water
in wild, wild places
that catches
grassroots.
We swallow the inheritance
of thick chops. Lick
the fat off our lips.
The hostage
takers of meat.
There is a fog
that fills the
lace frill of the
skull cap. Axons
dance. Dendrites
caresses the material
of space. Standing
there in a nice
dress the sea

foams out all
around me. Arranges
itself as if it
were light. It has
found the exit out
in much the same
way images, destinations,
conversations have. All
are intrigued by desire.
The tribe remains silent.
The rain smells like
burning wood. Driftwood.
The veld on fire.
The intent to flood,
to pour fluid/liquid
into something is

particularly there.
Heavy. This feeling
of ice remains. A fat
triumph that has found
the only possible exit
out. How can we stop
the moon from shining.
Its code.

Its light praiseworthy.
The stars can fill
walls at night
in my bedroom.
Stars are not part
of the stigmatized. The lonely.
Maps. They cannot
be found there.
The drought/famine.
They're only the cast
offs of the global
hierarchy. Science.
The flowers are stiff
and whimsical
in the breeze.
Bees are found
in that brain
fog. The future
is smiling at me. All of
superstitious
me. The universe is silent.
Traffic mysterious.
Its a blank space
of dry writing.

Melancholy
By Ryan Joel

At some point in your life. You meet someone. And through everything you've experienced. Or not experienced. This just seems right. It is that pursuit of happiness that drives us. Imbues us with that yearning. That pursuit of love. Sacred union. Oneness.

It is at that point when you decide to let it all go. To disrobe your past. And jump headlong into the nakedness of this new adventure. The most powerful force in the universe. It does that. Unashamedly pushing us to the edge of reason. And if you survive. You get to stand proud atop the cusp of forever. If not... Well..

If it beats you. Tears you apart. Then your scars will run deep. One too many times. They'll just get deeper. Until there is nothing left to cut through. Nothing left to instigate the pain. Just. Nothing.

Then you will truly be free. Because you will fear nothing. And the vestige of what you once were in love. Will sink to the depths of that cadaver you so reluctantly inhabit. Never to be found again. And that will be your fate.

There is no recipe for success. But only a hair trigger for failure. Much akin to dancing a jig through a minefield. What then are your chances for success? If at all any. Love is a nuclear device planted in your very soul. The radiation will feed you. But kill you in the end. Poison you. Slowly. Sometimes. The implosion is spectacular. But the aftermath less than elegant. There is no win.

It will be the one time in your life. You expose the shine of your soul. To another. They will admire it. Bask in its warmth. Or they will hack at it. And leave it patchy and broken. Staggered strands of light everywhere. And dark thoughts will hide in the patchy shadows. They will feed on your thoughts. They will grow until every last inkling of light has been extinguished.
And then. There is nothing. Just Nothing.
Only darkness. And that will be your solace.

Because in the dark. Nobody can see the tears that your soul cries.

Can I Walk Alongside?
By Charmane MacGregor

Can I walk alongside a while?
Not in your shoes for I have not the strength.
I promise not to tarry too long,
a moment on your journey is all I dare take.

Sympathy untainted by experience,
Each one a burden to bear.
My eyes blurred by your certain end I lose focus on mine nearer still.

Loneliness
By Megan Macleod

A loving family, plenty of friends
A place to live, and a nice warm bed

Yet here I sit with the demon drink
To numb the pain and void all emotion
But pain persists, and loneliness exists
As I sit in darkness pitying me

For loneliness is not exclusive you see
It takes hold any place, any where
distorts your mind with suicidal thoughts
blocking your sweet serenity

Grasping you and binding you
with disparate aloneness

The power to torment you
Distort your life and sanity

Reach out, shout for help
Have faith and believe

The line is fine
But people do care
Or so I hear.

The Disregarded Town
By Simon Wong

Much debris rolls through these city streets.
From the gutter, they trespass on paths
And shop doors like bandits,
Impeding the way of many
Who try to ignore the ramblings of passing filth.
Traders mop up the mess
That's always left behind.
To no avail, as more trash comes through the rank.
Tobacco ends, and empty bottles,
The stains upon the ground,
That cements a lasting image
Of the disregarded town.

Smoke billows from worn-out high-rises.
From grimy windows, the stench rips through
Seams in fabrics of stone,
Cutting through the smoggy skies,
Sewing sullen shapes onto black canvasses.
The mannequins' homes
Are left behind forgotten.
They strike careless poses, unobserved.
Looked at by none,
Overlooked by everyone;
The lasting image of a town
Seen by no one.

The mildew creeps from top to bottom.
From cracked hinges, the decaying door
Clings onto existence.
The decrepit man lies with it.
The first spirit to leave; the last body to go.
The syringe lies helpless,
Next to its patron, slouched,
And refuse leaks from every pore.
Roaches lie, and empty eyes,
The stains upon the ground.
That cements a lasting image
Of the disregarded town.

Trauma
By Gail Dendy

The city had emptied out for the summer and it seemed that I was alone, as if no one had ever lived in this place before. The sky opened at daylight and closed at sunset. The streets were heavy with trees, and, at alternating times, the trees were mirrors of colour. I was on vacation, and had nothing to do but examine the inner workings of my mind.

My mind, I say. Not my heart, for it is very little and too patched and worn to be of any great use. I am not speaking illness, here, but rather of what is commonly called *trauma*. The word itself harbours great openness, like that of a field which has no end but is peppered with yellow-flowering weeds, and at night it seems as though stars are silk-screened on to a single, wide expanse.

But with trauma arrived many other things, as though a procession of coaches was paraded before my very eyes: the coach of anger, russet-coloured, its paint artfully stressed; the coach of shock which is the colour of bandaged legs and feet. Oh, so many coaches, I no longer had sufficient names to name them, although I counted them as they slid through my brain, and wrote down the number and hid it for a while inside my pocket.

Some weeks later, I locked that number in the vault of my fist but, some days after that, I cast it upon a flame. By then the summer was over and the town began filling up again. The days now barked and howled; at night the restaurants were full and flashed red and blue and green with sports TVs. Beer cans opened. Wine was poured. Boerewors leaked fat on the very many grills.

Oh, it was just as before. But nothing was as it was. Overnight I had grown from child to woman. In a matter of hours I was married and divorced. The priest who'd blessed us had already died. My parents too were dead, and by their own hands. I had neither brother nor sister, aunt nor cousin.

It was at this point I took it into my head to learn to fly, and I *did* fly, clumsily at first, thrashing my arms upon the air but making little progress. Some thought me mad. Some offered me pills; others, wisdom; yet others, the infinite progress of silence. But I persevered, and on mornings when the oxblood sun had yet to rise, I would become airborne for perhaps an hour or so. But these were secret journeys, and always completed when the workday began.

These journeys became my life. I could see everything from a very great height. I could be godlike and discern the working cogs of the world it its entirety. And then I would descend into places of computers and printer-ink and grease, of house keys, access cards, traffic jams and petrol – these would become my Parliament. Many times, at night, the world that I had lost would be found again in little more than fountain-pen and paper. It was a language of largeness and largesse, of enemies now friends, of gold and silver chatter, of dance and music and tremendous art. Oh, I was so, so rich.

And then I awoke and, it being the middle of the night, I pulled the blankets further up upon my shoulders, swallowed another heart-shaped, stone-white pill, and fell asleep again.

Loneliness
By Guy Morris

Loneliness can be a state,
that some enjoy, but most of us hate!
Those who enjoy, call it solitude.
Others who don't, puts them in a mood.
It makes you beg the question why?
And all you want to do is cry!
How on earth, did it get like this?
I had a family and friends that I miss!
What did I do, that was so wrong?
I'm in a place, where I don't belong!
If you know someone who feels like this.
Give them a call, a hug, or a kiss.
To you, it means nothing, but easy to do.
You'll make their day! You know it's true.
They may be in a crowd, but can still feel alone.
So do it today, just pick up the phone.
No matter how busy you are with your everyday life!
Do it! You may even save someone's life.

Jigsaw Blues
By Cameron John Bryce

The jigsaw piece is puzzled;
He can't find the others.
But they are   here,
        there,
and
                    everywhere

        In between.

He knows they'll make a picture
of beauty bolder than the sea,
a story older than scripture,
If that moment could only be,

where
        every
                piece
                        alone
Comes together and makes a home.

Whenever You Behold
By James Scalise

Whenever I may chance to see
some special splendored view,
I stop.
And think of you.

And wish this day,
that all your days
be filled with rosy dawns
in crystal turquoise skies.

With rainbows round the mountain mists
and golden dusks which light the way
to gleaming diamond stars,
sparkling in your dream filled night.

In hope, wherever you may see
how wondrous all this beauty you behold,
you stop.
And also think of me.

And when at night In midst of sleep
you softly turn your head,
may your pillow seem to be
my waiting arms instead.

Then, may the lovely smile
which first made my heart yearn,
beam your glow into my dreams
and mine to yours in turn.

Indifference Of A Tree
By Alan Rorke

You face the water falling from above
But heedless of the salt pools on the ground
Grow branches upward, nestle dove
The fall of leaves my ears, my hair around.

My face upturned your boughs that block the blue,
A path that winds to dodge your selfish bark.
Standing slumber bare-stem snowfall. Who
Survives the winter, waiting out the dark?

Not me, but you. Your presence gives no gains
No warmth or respite from the beach of white.
Then sap that rises secret in your veins
Your springtime magic flowing up your height.

My jealous feet, your soil, your hidden roots
My calloused hands, your supple summer shoots.

Silent Prayers
By Karishma Krishna Kumar

"Shhhhhhh", the wind lashed against the tree branch, that was precariously dangling; half hanging, half attached to the bark of the tree.

She cracked her knuckles as she contemplated the whispers that hissed relentlessly, pouring venom into her ears. Her ear canal hungrily drank in the venom, her middle ear absorbed the poison and her inner ear digested the toxin, letting out a resonating belch.

"Grief", she typed into a new tab on Google Chrome. A basic definition of the emotions that were coursing through her veins popped up on her screen. Yes! It was a multifaceted response. YES! The knot in her stomach had physical, cognitive, behavioural, social, and philosophical dimensions. YES!

An odd sense of relief engulfed the tips of her fingers as she realised that she wasn't alone; someone, somewhere, in the world had at some point felt all the feelings that were throbbing underneath the skin of her chest; somewhere near her heart.

The ocean of her melancholy, gurgled under the gravitational forces of the sun and the moon. Tides rose, and waves of the blue devils came rushing at her and died at her feet. She gathered them with both hands and kissed the elixir of life back into them until the blue funk was resuscitated. The moon inched closer and she felt the lunar lunacy grab her shins. She buckled; and fell down to her knees. The waters wet the seams of her clothes and permeated into her pores.

The orifice on her wrist began draining the torment of her aching heart into the briny deep. "What do I do with his love?", she bellowed to the silent night sky. "Nothing, it'll haunt you all on its own", the full moon replied. She gave into the throes of the Transylvania effect as it enslaved her deepest core. "I can't un-love him", she murmured to her inner being. "He made me ... me .. I am me, but me is part him", eyes half closed, half open, she and placed herself in the lotus position imitating Lord Shiva when He was grieving.

The first flush of morning found her still; un-moving. Her silence had consumed her pain and dissipated it. Dawn found her as if nothing had happened; because in truth nothing had happened, to her. Nothing ever happens to anyone. Grief, depression, blues are like the tides; they rise and fall. But, the soul is untouched, unmoved, unfeeling. She stayed in her space of Zen until the fishermen came to catch the morning fry. She got up and went back home; healed yet not. How can one be healed, when essentially, they were never broken? The night had passed; and with it, so had her misery.

Smoking
By Simon Atkin

This room is so still
and memories cut
through me as words
sometimes do
hanging above my feeble
smile
I can no longer wish
to be anywhere
neither here nor there
for this room stays so
cold and so bare
The sun shone upon
the fireplace
I lit a cigarette
Which I love
Then for no good reason
My whole world died
I look for a friend
I'm feeling so lonely today

Loneliness At Work
By Dawa Rinzin

I do not know what I feel
Neither am I aware nor am I clear
Do, what I do?
All again it is a doubt
What do I do every day?
The game of this period
Played to waste our times; precious though,
I am not sure
If I am sad or happy
All ever, along the journey; routine
The same work till today
Future tiresome ahead
Memories exhausting behind
I have done nothing, the same thing,
Yet everything changed in glimpse.

All Alone
By Gayathri Viswanath

One by one, they all left
It was just me now
All of a sudden, I felt bereft
To pick myself up, I never knew how
He was always there;
My strong pillar of support
With him gone forever
There was no more purport
The nights were going to be tough
The empty bed will say it all
Cannot convince the heart enough
When the ears will hear him call
People say with time
The pain does heal
But it is in his absence
His presence I feel.

Hello, Goodbye
By Rohini Sunderam

Some day you will go
And it will be like your coming
The indifferent hello
When we met.

All hellos are the beginnings
Of all goodbyes.

But we stepped forward
Into the stream of the future
Into hello and goodbye
And into farewell

Long before farewell
Meant anything but
Hello.

Contributors...

Abigail George
Abigail is a blogger on Goodreads, a short story writer, a feminist, and a full-time poet. She is hard at work on a young adult novel. She briefly studied speech and drama and film. She was the recipient of writing grants from the National Arts Council in Johannesburg, Centre for the Book in Cape Town, and the Eastern Cape Provincial Arts and Culture Council in East London, South Africa. Her literary work (fiction) was nominated for the Pushcart Prize. She lives in the Eastern Cape, South Africa. She has been published widely in print and online in South Africa, as well as abroad and has written for *Modern Diplomacy* and contributed to a symposium on *Ovi Magazine*: Finland's English Online Magazine.
E: abigailgeorge79@gmail.com

Alistair Baptista
For more nomadic chaos...
E: alistairbaptista@gmail.com
W: Talkingcomix.wordpress.com

Alan Murphy
Alan is the Irish writer and illustrator of three collections of poetry for young readers. Dublin-born, he currently lives in Lismore, county Waterford. His latest collection, *Prometheus Unplugged*, was listed in a children's and young adults' books of the year article in the *Irish Times*. He has been featured in children's poetry anthologies in the UK and America. "A lot of incredible talent has emerged recently from Ireland. Alan Murphy is one of the them." - Anastasia Gonis, *Buzz Words* magazine.
E: alanmu@eircom.net
W: Avantcardpublications.com

Alan Rorke
Alan resides in Cape Town, where he is inspired by both the rhythms of nature and the effect of society on basic human nature. He has a great love for literature, and his poetry alternates between an adherence to classical form and frees verse.
E: alan.rorke@gmail.com

Anna Cheung
Anna Cheung currently lives in Glasgow in bonnie Scotland. Her writing repertoire includes published online music reviews for new independent music; blogs for the arts and heritage project, *A View*

from Here (Refugee Week Scotland) and had one of her poems,*Thirst* published in the e-magazine, *Dark Eclipse*. Her new project is writing children's picture books.
E: dollynoodle@googlemail.com

Ashraf Booley
Ashraf is a young digital content producer and poet living and working in Cape Town. He's always on the lookout for the next big food trend and loves cooking and penning poetry in his spare time. His poetry has been published online by *Aerodrome, Botsotso, Badilisha Poetry X-Change, Word n Sound* and *Poetry Potion*, as well as literary journals *New Contrast* and *New Coin* (to be published in June 2016). His first published poem appeared in the *UWC Creates* anthology; *This is my Land,* compiled by Antjie Krog, Meg vanderMerwe and Sindiwe Magona. Ashraf also enjoys taking photographs and is passionate about human rights and equality.
E: booley.ash@gmail.com

Bernard Levinson
Bernard is a Psychiatrist/Sexologist with a practice in Johannesburg, South Africa. His works have been published in a number of publications, the most important for him are his four volumes of poetry currently taught in Gauteng schools.
E: levinson@iburst.co.za

Cameron John Bryce
"I am Cameron John Bryce. I am twenty two year old student, musician, and helpless rambler from Glasgow. I can be found wandering around South street on the banks of the Clyde and muttering to myself. When I'm not in one of those moods, I write things. They are often strange."
E: cameron@freshbs.com

Chandra Gurung
"I am from Nepal, currently working with a contracting company in The Kingdom of Bahrain. I write in my native language Nepali. I have an anthology of poetry in my credit and am planning for my second anthology soon."
E: chandu_901@hotmail.com

Charmane MacGregor
"Jaded battle-weary lawyer, mother of two small children, with a commercial helicopter pilot's license to prove I really can be all that I can... closet hermit longing for the simple life with time to contribute something worthwhile, wife of a saint for having stayed married to

me."
E: Charmane@meattorneys.co.za

Christine Mcleod
Currently based in New Zealand, Christine has a diploma in holistic life coaching and, over the years, has worked with people who suffer from mental illness, which she found extremely rewarding and opened her eyes to the heartache and struggle that comes with mental illness. Although, while in high-school, she had a couple of poems published in local publications, her real interest in writing and poetry came recently while travelling in Thailand and meeting up with a freelance journalist. Since then she has been inspired to develop her literary skills in both poetry and prose.
E: mcleod02@xtra.co.nz

Claudia Hardt
Claudia is a PR-Consultant certified by the German Academy of Public Relations in Frankfurt and holds a Bachelor of Arts in Hotel Business Management. She has 26 years experience in the tourism industry and agency business, of which she has spent 17 years in public relations and communications. She discovered writing as a teenager, and was the first female deputy editor of her high-school magazine, where she was lucky enough to win a high-school magazine competition in the Federal State of North Rhine-Westphalia, Germany, where she lived at that time. While studying in Heidelberg, her passion for writing and publishing developed even further with the opportunity to manage a monthly students' magazine, a yearbook, and to regularly contribute to various hospitality magazines. Having travelled extensively around the world and, over the past 20 years, lived and worked in different regions including Europe, Asia and the Middle East, Claudia regularly used her passion for adventurous trips and photography to create travel stories and columns which have been published in places such as Malaysia, Hong Kong, Cyprus, Bahrain and Germany. Apart from that she is a contributor to the following anthologies; *More of My Beautiful Bahrain, Poetic Bahrain* and *What Women Really Want*.
E: claudiahardt@hotmail.de
W: Bahrainwriterscircle.wordpress.com/our-members/claudia-hardt

Courtney Speedy
Courtney is a 18 year old poet from Whangarei, New Zealand. She has had her poetry published in two separate collections; *Re-Draft: The Word Is Out* (2014) and *Write Off Line: They Came in From the Dark* (2014) Her inspiration comes from the world around her and music in particular. She is working towards self-publishing a

collection of her poetry and prose in the near future.
E: courtneyleoniejayne@gmail.com

David Hollywood
David is Irish and married with four children and has been an enthusiastic poet all of his life. His particular interest is in developing a public enthusiasm for poetry among those who aspire but to, but haven't yet made the leap into proclaiming their verse. As a result, he has hosted and directed *The Colours of Life* poetry festivals in both Bahrain and latterly in Ireland, which are targeted towards showcasing on stage the personal script and efforts of citizens who might not otherwise have a chance to receive acknowledgements for their creativity. As a consequence, the festival in Bahrain is now among the largest poetry activities in The Gulf Region of The Middle East. David is the author of an eclectic collection of poems titled *Waiting Spaces*, plus contributor to *My Beautiful Bahrain, Poetic Bahrain, More of My Beautiful Bahrain*, and is the in-house poet for *Bahrain Confidential* magazine and, as a result, he is one of the most widely read Western poets in The Middle East. He is also a regular literary critic for *Taj Mahal Review* plus an essayist on the subject of poetry appreciation. There are plans for a new collection of poetry and essays to be released in 2017.
E: davidhollywood23@hotmail.com

Dawa Rinzin
"I was born in a small Asian country called Bhutan. I usually write when I am alone, because most of my life I have spent alone with my ageing parents, which has made me write up my feelings and express them."
E: rigzindawa2016@gmail.com

Douglas Bruton
Douglas throws words together. Sometimes they make sense and sometimes they even make stories. He sends those thrown-together words out to nice places and every now and then that makes sense, too. He thinks he is a writer, but that's just more words that he throws about. He has been published in many nice places, including *The Eildon Tree, Transmission, The Delinquent, Grasslimb Journal, The Blood Orange Review, The Vestal Review, Storyglossia, Ranfurly Review, The Smoking Poet, Interpreter's House, Flash Magazine, Brittle Star Magazine* and *Fiction Attic Press*. He has also won more than a handful of writing competitions including *HISSAC, Firstwriter, Biscuit* and *Brighter Writers Circle Prize*. And if that's not enough, he has had recognition from *The Bridport Prize*, and *Fish*, and *The Sean O'Faolain Competition*. He has a children's novel in print, too. And

that's why he thinks he must be a writer. It seems that if you throw enough words down on paper then some of them amount to something.
E: douglasrdbruton@hotmail.com

Dilraz AR Kunnummal
Born and brought up in Bahrain, Dilraz has always had a penchant for writing. Armed with a Bachelors in Business Administration and a Masters in Broadcast Journalism, she has worked in Mumbai for a while before moving back to Bahrain. Over the last two years, she has worked with *Signature Bahrain*, the *Daily Tribune* and as the editor for *Sabaya Magazine*. She is an avid reader, a trained Indian classical dancer and choreographer, and is on the continuous journey to dabble in her passions; finding fun, knowledge and smiles along the way.
E: dilraz@gmail.com

Farha A. Jaleel
"I was born and brought up in Bahrain. I currently live in Sri Lanka. I started out writing short stories at the age of eight and have been passionate about it ever since. I started writing poems a few years ago. I have had one of my short stories published in a local newspaper in Sri Lanka, and I hope to get more of my work published in the future."
E: crimson_rose97@yahoo.com

Gail Dendy
South African writer Gail is the author of seven collections of poetry published in Britain, South Africa and the United States respectively. She has the unique distinction of having been published by Nobel Prizewinner Harold Pinter, and of sharing a poetry collection with Peabody Winner and Oscar Nominee Norman Corwin. Gail's writing is diverse: she won the *SA PEN Millennium* playwriting competition; shared the monetary prize for the Herman Charles Bosman Award (poetry); was shortlisted for the Thomas Pringle Award (short story) and the Sol Plaatje/European Union Poetry Prize; was longlisted for *Short Story Day Africa* and the *Twenty in 20 Project* (featuring the best twenty stories written in English since the inception of South Africa's democracy); and gained 'Highly Commended' in the Poetry Space Competition 2014 (UK) ('Commended' for 2015) and for the Dinaane Debut Fiction Award (for an unpublished novel). Most recently, *Ruminations on the Plum* was featured by Trevor Conway (Galway, Ireland) in *Poems in Profile* (March 2016), while her poem *Suitcase* was featured in the profile of Gail Dendy – Author as included in the KZN Literary Tourism Project. Gail lives in

Johannesburg and works as a Library & Research Manager for an international corporate-law firm.
E: gmdendy@iafrica.com

Gayathri Viswanath
"I am Gayathri. I am an Indian national living in Bahrain for the past 8 years and hopefully for many more years to come. I am a homemaker and a mother of a very inquisitive six year-old and a hyperactive 20 months-old. I love reading fiction, especially the genres of thrillers, mystery, romance and humour. It always amazes me to see how well an author puts his thoughts to paper and this has inspired me to write. I firmly believe that everyone has a story to tell and I hope to tell mine to the world one day. This poem is dedicated to my mother and I have tried to capture her feelings when my dad passed away unexpectedly five years ago."
E: gayathri113@gmail.com

Grace Ebbey
Grace is an 18 year old author, who's in love with sad stories and Johannesburg. She's been writing for as long as she can remember and published her book on Kindle in 2014. Like a writer, she's obsessed with coffee, music and people. And the complexities of human emotion.
E: graceebbey1@gmail.com

Guy Morris
Guy was born in Yorkshire 1962 and, after a multitude of jobs since leaving school, he has worked in transport for the past thirty years, carrying both passengers and heavy goods far and wide. During his travels, seeing all kinds of things to do with life, he's noticed that loneliness appears in many forms and thinks that for some it's a taboo subject and isn't mentioned enough.
FB: Facebook.com/MaurizzioCasabianco

Heidi Al Khajah
Heidi is a talented, results-producing publishing and marketing professional with over 15 years experience in her field, with a BA in Publishing. Her career includes publishing, graphic design, marketing and corporate communications, working in the fields of telecom, advertising, aviation and real estate. She recently contributed to the editing team of *The Torch Principle*.
E: layle@mail.com
LinkedIn: Bh.linkedin.com/pub/heidi-al-khajah/3/669/b25

Ian McKenzie

Ian has contributed to poetry anthologies celebrating Luddism and ephemera. He has poetry published in Glasgow's *Raum Magazine*, and his hatred of modern life included in the March 2016 *Lies, Dreaming* monthly podcast. He refuses to mention this poem by its title so a certain giant Scandinavian furniture chain doesn't get free advertising.
E: ian_j_mckenzie@hotmail.co.uk

Irwin Rego

A Bombay born Canadian residing in Bahrain, Irwin is a creative communications professional whose forte is copy and content development, marketing and branding. A disciple of intuitive ideation and judgemental design thinking, he is a fun-loving simple guy - an inquisitorial wanderer who is constantly seeking to transcend the reasoning and imagination realm for answers that connect mind, heart and soul. Likes to see himself as a 'HEARTIST' - his creative ideas and insights have helped corporations and individuals build and enhance their brand image and reputation, driving revenues. He has weaved stories and ideas for his clients across the Middle East. He also is a prolific writer of inspiring and thought provoking articles and poetry on his blog He believes in 'living the life' and contributing his part to the Universe in a small way, even if at times it means disturbing the sleep of status quo's sentinels, or upsetting the worshippers of the obtuse thinking gods.
E: irwinrego@gmail.com
Blog: Articlewalla.blogspot.com.

James Scalise

Jim is enjoying a life's goal in retirement of writing full time. Architecture, teaching and lecturing have taken him across the US, and through the Middle East to train their architects, engineers and teachers. His published works include numerous presentations and books on the art of teaching, a lengthy essay on Bahrain architecture in *My Beautiful Bahrain*, and the poem *A Conversation in Bahrain* in *My Poetic Bahrain*. Jim is an active member of the Writers' League of Texas and the Society of Children's Book Writers and Illustrators.
E: Jim.Scalise@gmail.com
E: jim.scalise@gmail.com

J D Trejo-Maya

Born in Celaya, Guanajuato, Mexico, where he spent his childhood in the small neighbouring rural pueblo of Tarimoro. Later JD immigrated in 1988 with his family to the United States, where he would go on to earn three degrees. In writing in particular his inspirations include the

ancient poet Netzahualcoyotl, contemporary Humberto Ak'abal and the *Gros Ventre/Blackfeet* novelist James Welch. He has been published in the *Nimrod International Poetry Journal*, *Belleville Park Pages*, *Star 82 Review*, *Visions International Review*, *Lost Coast Review*, *Redactions: Poetry & Poetics*, *Altadena Poetry Review (2015 & 2016)*, *Acentos Review*, *Mandala Journal*, *Five Quarterly*, *Qua Quarterly*, *The Voices Project*, *Turtle Island Quarterly*, *Taj Mahal Review*, *Constellations*, *Dukool*, *Solstice Literary Magazine*, *In Stereo Press*, and *Stone Bird Anthology of the Eagle Rock Library*. Here, including a nomination for the Pushcart Prize 2015 by Redactions: Poetry & Poetics. While in ceremony with Chololo medicine men in the Tule River Reservation he dreamt the above written prophecy...
E: jdtrejomaya@gmail.com

Lonita Nugrahayu
Born and growing up in Jakarta, Indonesia, Lonita is a home-maker now residing in the Kingdom of Bahrain. She finds writing therapeutic, and has been writing poetry on and off since childhood. At the moment she is focusing on polishing her work, but one day wishes to have her work published, as well as introducing poetry to younger generation as part of encouraging them to have more respect for the literary world. She also hopes to inspire and encourage other women to take up the pen and shape words into poems. She believes the best words are those that come from the heart.
E: lonitaan@outlook.com
FB: Facebook.com/lonita.bilal

Karishma Krishna Kumar
Karishma is a freelance writer from India and has completed a Bachelor of Arts degree in English Literature from the University of Pune. As an avid traveller, she draws inspiration from the lives of people she's met during her explorations of the underbelly of her country. Raised in the Kingdom of Saudi Arabia and an introvert during her childhood years, she holds the subject of loneliness and being alone very close to her heart. She has no previous publications and expects to release her first novel in the next few months.
E: karishmakrishnakumar@gmail.com
W: Karishmakrishnakumar.com
Blog: morning-fire.blogspot.com

Kathleen Boyle
Kathleen Boyle *nee* Dodd, was born in Liverpool, where she spent her childhood years before leaving to train as a teacher in Hull in 1972. Kathleen has worked as a teacher in Hull, Leeds and Carlisle and

international schools in Columbia, Bahrain and Cairo. She has written stories and poems throughout her life, publishing a collection of poems about growing up in 1950s Liverpool entitled, *Sugar Butties and Mersey Memoirs* as well as a collection of poems for children about a teddy bear called *Harry Pennington*. During her time in Bahrain she wrote *The Pearl House* a short story which spans the cultural divides of Liverpool and Bahrain. The story, together with her poems, *Bahrain* and *Umm Al Hassam* were published in the collections, *My Beautiful Bahrain* and *More of My Beautiful Bahrain*. Kathleen has written a series of childrens' stories for Beirut publishers Dar El Fikr, two of which, *The Jewel of the Deep* and *The Magic Pearl and Dilmun*, have now been illustrated and published. She has written a novella, *Catherine of Liverpool,* and is presently working on the sequel. Now into her fortieth year as a teacher, she combines her love of travel with teaching and is presently based in Cairo, Egypt.
E: kathdodd@aol.com

Keith Nunes
Keith is from Lake Rotoma, New Zealand. He was a newspaper sub-editor for 20-plus years but after a nervous breakdown he moved into rural squalor and writes for the sheer joy of it. He's been published around NZ and increasingly in the UK and US. He is a *Pushcart Prize* nominee and his chapbook *Crashing the Calliope* is sold by the lunatic fringe.
E: kwn@ihug.co.nz

Lucy Reid
Lucy found writing at 14, when her first real story was read aloud. A stuffed full car ride several years later, would take her to the literary heart of Edinburgh. There her calling to write grew. Here she found herself in poetry, even performed her first reading. Dipped into her first ever screenplay. Dived into her first-love – prose. Now she spends her time searching the city for stories, and carries a little teal notepad wherever she goes.
E: lucyalannareid@gmail.com
Blog: Theimperfectreader.wordpress.com

Lynda Chouiten
Lynda teaches literature at the Department of Foreign Languages of the University of Boumerdes (Algeria). She is the editor of a volume entitled *Commanding Words: Essays on the Discursive Constructions, Manifestations, and Subversions of Authority* (Newcastle: Cambridge Scholars Publishing, 2016) and the author of *Isabelle Eberhardt and North Africa: A Carnivalesque Mirage* (Lanham, MD: Lexington Books, 2015) as well as of several articles pertaining to culture and literary

criticism. Lynda writes poems in English and fiction in French – she has just completed one full-length novel. She is also interested in literary translation. Her major current project consists in translating into English the poems of Si Mohand U'Mhand, a nineteenth-century nomadic Berber poet.
E: chouiten_lynda@yahoo.fr

Lynda Jessen-Tye
Lynda has had articles published locally and writes short stories and poetry. She wrote a column for two years for her local Parent Centre's Newsletter called *New Mum On The Block*. She has entered several short story competitions and won one in 2012 with her story *Early Morning*. In 2016 she started entering poetry competitions. She lives in sunny Nelson in New Zealand with her husband, eleven year old daughter, a dog, a cat and three tropical fish. She is a part-time early childhood teacher.
E: lyndajessentye@gmail.com

Lynda Tavakoli
Lynda hails from Northern Ireland where she teaches special needs and facilitates several adult creative writing classes. She is the author of two novels, and her short stories have appeared both in print and on BBC Radio Ulster and RTE. As a freelance journalist she has had a variety of human interest and travel pieces published in the International Press. Lynda's poems have been included in a wide range of publications including Templar Poets' Anthology *Skein*, Abridged *Absence / Magnolia / Silence / Primal / Mara*, *The Incubator Journal*, Listowel Winners' Anthology, Panning for Poems Poetry *NI and Circle and Square*, Fiery Arrow Press. She was selected as *The Irish Times*, Hennessy poet of the month for October 2015, and has recently seen her work published in *The Weekender* magazine, Bahrain. She is presently working on putting together a poetry collection reflecting her upbringing in Northern Ireland.
E: lyndatavakoli@aol.com

Madhavi Dwivedi
"My first rendezvous with writing was at college. My scribbling, which I fondly called 'poems', was proudly and regularly passed on to the like-minded class-mates. We would exchange the little slips, dubbing them 'data' in the psychology class and savour each other's badly cooked write-ups. After about four years of such expressions of passionate thoughts, there came a grand lull in my writing. Laundry lists, love and hate letters replaced all that writer's pride 'data'. It took a decade for me to pick up writing again with zeal and zest. As a result, in the past few years I have written about 50 articles which

were published in the editorial columns. I have written as many poems most of which are still hatching in the warmth of my private closet. Hope one day, I will feel ready to share them with the world. My articles were invariably written when I hungered to share my thoughts with the world. However, most of my poems were the direct consequence of some kind of personal flood happening in my heart. Hence, their fate generally was the bottom folder in my personal closet. I contributed to *My Beautiful Bahrain*, *More of My Beautiful Bahrain* and *Poetic Bahrain* as well. My most cherished aspiration is publishing a joint book of my daughter's and my write-ups. A subsidiary dream - life permitting - is to write a book which could summarize my life's emotions in the form of a story that will leave the readers with a smile in their heart and with a storm in their minds.
E: madhavi.dwivedi@gmail.com

Maire Malone
"I was born and raised in Dublin and emigrated to the UK in the '80s. Over the years I have written poetry, articles and more recently fiction. I have had several poems published and selected in competitions and won first prize in an *Anthology of Poems in Memory of Freda Downie* (Ver Poets). When my first two short stories were accepted for publication and won prizes, I decided to perfect my craft further and devote more time to writing. I have participated in many writing courses in London; City Lit, The University of Hertfordshire and an Arvon Course. I am currently writing my first novel.
E: maireowens@aol.com

Maren Bodenstein
Marengrew up in a small village in Kwa Zulu Natal in South Africa. She has written for children, produced a story for BBC Radio 4 and has published a novel called *Shooting Snakes*.
E: marenbody@gmail.com

Margaret Clough
Margaret is a retired Soil Chemist and Science teacher. She has had poems and short stories published in various journals and contributed to the collection of plays for schools *Short, Sharp and Snappy* edited by Robin Malan. She is the author of two collections of poems: *At Least the Duck Survived* and *The Last to Leave*. both published by Modjaji Books.
E: margieclough@webmail.co.za

Mary Burgerhout
Mary, originally from the Outer Hebrides, is a member of Huntly

Writers in the North-East of Scotland. She writes occasional verse in both English and in her native language of Gaelic.
E: maryburgerhout979@btinternet.com

Megan MacLeod
"I am Megan MacLeod, novice poet, rambler of ideas and scribbler of thoughts. My private writing comprises of poems (or musings and rambling with ink to parchment). On a professional note, since 2002 I have written news releases, content for websites, client profiles, edited articles and features, and created tag-lines and body copy for advertising."
E: macleodmegan@hotmail.com

Nilanjana Bose
Nilanjana is a parent, writer, poet, blogger and a market research professional. Born in Kolkata, India, brought up in New Delhi and West Africa, her mailing address has changed some 15 times so far and she is always ready for the next change. She believes in travelling light, and a sense of humour, along with the passport, is top on her packing list. Dipping into other cultures and countries, whether as an expat resident or a tourist, refreshes her writing muscles. She speaks English, Bengali and Hindi; and understands more Arabic than she can account for. She has a first class degree in Maths from Delhi University, a diploma in Marketing from Chartered Institute of Marketing, UK; and has lived/worked in India, Nigeria, Bahrain, UAE and Egypt. She celebrates the diverse range of cultural environments that she has experienced and her ability to navigate different landscapes of language, beliefs and customs. She has written over 2000 poems, 100s of short stories, flash fiction and essays, her writing is informed by her travels as well as her own heritage. Her poems, short stories, essays and travel memoirs have been published in both print and on-line. Her first book was a collection of short fiction in Bengali called *Seemaheen Bidesh (Foreign without Borders)*. Her work has appeared in print in *Ananda Lipi* (US), *Sabaya* (Bahrain), in multi-author anthologies like *Social Potpourri – An Anthology* and *10 Love Stories* released by Indiblogger and Harper Collins India in 2015, as well as online in e-zines like *eFiction India*. She was a contributing editor in *Inner Child* magazine (US) with her own byline *Passport to Our World* a travel feature which ran to a 24 part series.
E: nilabose306b@gmail.com
Blog: Madly-in-Verse

Omar Ahmed
Omar Ahmed Khulaqi (OAK) is a young poet of terror and romance

from Yemen, raised in Bahrain. He is highly influenced by Edgar Allan Poe and the poetry of the Romantic era. His poems made way to local magazines and even an anthology called *My Beautiful Bahrain* and its follow up *More of My Beautiful Bahrain* along with a short story. His work uses dark, melodramatic themes of tension and awakening induced by fear and trembling. Recent works deal with subjects of spiritual enlightenment layered in surrealism.
E: oaky_66@outlook.com
Instagram: B.t.oaktree
FB: Beneath the Oak Tree

Robert Hirschfield
"I am a New York-based poet and travel writer. My poems have appeared in magazines such as *Salamander*, *Tablet* and *Pamplemousse* in the United States, *Descant* in Canada and *European Judaism* in the United Kingdom. I also review books of poetry and do feature pieces on poets for various publications, including *Sojourners* in the United States and *Kindred Spirit* in the United Kingdom. Some of my travel writing, which consists mostly of India stories, belong to a category I call *Travelling With Poets*. I will take the poetry of the great African-American poet, Lucille Clifton, for example, and 'travel' with it through the years of racism in America that I grew up with."
E: bobbyhirschfield@gmail.com

Rohini Sunderam
Rohini is a semi-retired advertising copywriter whose articles have been published in *The Statesman*, Calcutta, India, *The Globe & Mail*, Canada, and *The Halifax Chronicle Herald*, Nova Scotia, Canada. As Zohra Saeed, she is the author of *Desert Flower* (Ex-L-Ence Publishing UK). She was a contributor to the anthology *My Beautiful Bahrain*, *More of My Beautiful Bahrain*, *Poetic Bahrain*, and *Corpoetry* – a collection of poems satirising corporate life. A poem was selected for publication in the international competition Poetry Rivals 2012. A story: *Your rebirth, My death*, placed 5th from 179 entries in the Atlantis Short Story contest 2013. She has presented her poetry in the annual *Colours of Life* Poetry Festival in Bahrain in 2012, 2013 and 2015.
E: RohiniSunderam@hotmail.com
Blog: Fictionpals.wordpress.com
FB: Facebook.com/RohiniSunderamAuthor/

Rosie Mapplebeck
Rosie is a traditional oral storyteller and heritage trail officer. She loves telling tales to a mixed age audience where families and friends share together. She writes poetry and short stories, performing at

slams and literary events. She hosts live literary events in Ayr and takes story walks round Ayrshire including Burns' Cottage in Alloway. Many of her stories and poems are from her deep experience of living among animals and birds and of magic. She co-owns a boarding cattery, offering holistic and healing care for animals. She studied botany with David Bellamy, has been a Special Constable, Veterinary Nurse and once ran a heavy metal disco. She is part of the delightful Living Voices project which brings story, song and poetry to elders and those with dementia. These days you are likely to find her creating poetry around Ayrshire where she lives or foraging wild plants for gastronomic delights. She's also a carer for our bees.
W: Rosiemapplebeck.co.uk
FB: Facebook.com/rosie.mapplebeck

Ryan Joel
Ryan is 39 and as well as being an artist, he has a profound love affair with writing and literature in general. Though he has no formally published works. His love for prose and short musings are deep and thought provoking. He is passionate about pushing the boundaries of imagination and toying with the human condition. You have been warned.
E: rjoel@mweb.co.za
Twitter: @Captainrawrsome

Sally Spedding
Born in Wales, Sally is a well-published crime/thriller writer. Her short stories and poetry have also been regularly published and won several major awards, including the H.E Bates Short Story Prize and the Anne Tibble Award for Poetry. She has won and been shortlisted for the Aesthetica Poetry Prize, the Bridport Prize, and many others. Twice a winner of the Anglo-Welsh International Poetry Competition, her latest work is in *Poetry Salzburg Review 28*.
W: www.sallyspedding.com

Sameer Qamar
Sameer, a Bahraini national, is a member of The Bahrain Writers' Circle, the biggest writer's group in Bahrain, and is a particularly active member of its sister group The Second Circle which deals exclusively with poetry. Sameer has a body of poetic work which consists of more than three dozen poems, covering topics as simple as a lazy morning drive to something as controversial as musings on the popular cultural zeitgest. He has taken part in a number of public poetry performances in Bahrain including the *Colours Of Life* festival, one of the most popular poetic fixtures in Bahrain's cultural events calendar. A number of his poems have been published collections of

literature centred around Bahrain entitled *More of My Beautiful Bahrain* and *Poetic Bahrain*.
E: sameerleo@hotmail.com

Sara Spivey
Originally from London, Sara spent a number of years working in advertising, marketing and training in the West End before moving to Hong Kong as Associate VP for ESPN TV. She fell in love with the Far East and its emerging artwork scene, so when she relocated to Phoenix, Arizona in 2000, the US restrictions whilst waiting for her green card, propelled her to start her own business. This she did, becoming an independent art dealer specialising in Vietnamese paintings and Chinese sculpture, which was well received by the US and European markets. After spending 10 years in America she returned to the UK for a short period before moving to Egypt three years ago working as a teacher in Cairo. She comes from a small family of journalists and published authors, publishing her own first novel in 2012 called *The Dragon of Hidden Treasures* aimed at the pre-teen market. Prior to this she had always focused on short story writing which she still loves creating. She currently has her second book *The Starbucks Soap* sketched out.
E: sara_sparky@email.com

Shirley Sampson
"Born in Sheffield, I reached Glasgow, my home now, via York, Liverpool, Dortmund, London, Salisbury and other places along the way. In my student days I was a canteen and shop assistant, potato-picker, dish-washer, laundry presser and shampoo girl before qualifying to teach. Early exposure to the British Army as wife of a squaddie who became an officer taught me a lot about hypocrisy and discrimination, and I was soon to add homelessness, divorce and poverty to my list of experiential learning. Meanwhile, being married on and (mostly) off, I brought up three children while working full-time in the public sector where I became an elected trade union official. In that role I was proud to instigate, plan and help deliver a workplace nursery, although since management set the fees, like many others, I could not afford to use it. However I constantly thank my stars that I was lucky enough to have benefited from an excellent grammar school education and loving parents, which provided me with the personal resources to cope with life's ups and downs. Recently I have enjoyed mining some of my experiences for my poetry."
E: bingalum@gmail.com

Simon Atkin
Simon started writing in the '90s, when he travelled within Eastern Europe and Switzerland, and to India and China. Unfortunately some 200 poems of his were lost in Paris, never to be found! Now residing in Leicestershire, UK, Simon is now a clock restorer and a butler, and working on a book about his travels and life in hospitality.
E: jeevesclocks@gmail.com

Simon Wong
Descended from refugees who fled the Vietnam War, Simon was born and raised in Edinburgh, Scotland. After graduating from The University of Edinburgh in 2013 with a degree in Philosophy and English Literature, he went on to write articles for magazines and newspapers in the UK and China. Simon enjoys writing on themes of identity, alterity, and place, and is the author of *Hugo and the Janus* (2016), a coming of age novella inspired by the fairy tale genre, available worldwide via Amazon. Simon is currently writing his debut novel, *The Mudskippers*, as well as a collection of vignettes entitled, *The Fragments of Hideyoshi Nakamura*, which is inspired by real events.
E: simonwong@live.co.uk
Instagram: __simonwong
Blog: scriptanime.com

Stu Armstrong
Stu Armstrong is an author from the North East of England who has had a number of books published and has recently turned his attention to poetry. Currently he has written two poetry books; *Life* and *Second Life*. Written towards the more modern contemporary end of the scale, Stu writes from the heart using real life experience.
W: Stuarmstrong.com

Toni Curran
Toni grew up on the beautiful Northern Beaches of Sydney, Australia. Gaining work experience in a wide range of industries and roles such as; an Executive Assistant, IT Sales Consultant, Real Estate Residential Sales Specialist, Business Development Manager, Security Personnel and now as a Funeral Director/Arranger/Conductor and mortuary assistant. Although she doesn't write much, she loves it when she does. Now in her mid 40s, Toni continues on her path of self discovery, learning about life and its myriad of lessons.
E: chileezz1@live.com.au

Tyrrel Francis
Tyrrel was born in Northamptonshire in 1975, and spent his early

school years in Avonmouth, and secondary school years in Hampshire, joining the Royal Navy in 1991. A keen Martial Artist since the age of 13, Tyrrel has always based most of his writing subject matter around this, whether that be his book *Personal Safety & Self Defence*, or his upcoming novel *Blood, Sweat & Tears*. Poetry has always been another love of his, and has recognised the need to be diverse as a writer, and the use of poetry both as an exercise in description and diversity, and a satisfying outlet for emotions and thoughts.
E: calmlymode@yahoo.co.uk

Vaijayantee Bhattacharya
Vaijayantee is an editor and writer with over 12 years of editorial experience in the print and publishing media. She is currently associated as Editor of a few well-known magazines and publications. A poet at leisure, several poems of hers have been published in various publications and she is currently working at her own anthology of poems.
E: vaijayantee@gmail.com
W: Teatalkwithvaijayantee.weebly.com

Zahra Zuhair
"My first poem came to me when I was 14 years old. Since then, I have found much inspiration in the works of great poets and writers, most specifically Shelley, Rilke and Toni Morrison. They have moved me, captured me and freed me. Ten years later, I can say I have written all sorts of things, some I no longer have and some I love dearly. However, all of what I have written, whether good or bad, carries so much meaning to me, and I only hope that one day my writing will be as meaningful to someone else."
E: zahrazuhair.91@gmail.com
FB: Facebook.com/zahra.zuhair.39
Blog: Keeeptalking.wordpress.com

Are You A Writer And/Or Poet?

I am looking for contributions from writers and poets, any age and from anywhere in the world, who feel they might like to contribute (in English) to one or more of our unique collections of poetry and short prose on particular topics and themes. No word count for poetry, maximum 1500 words for short prose. You can write under your real name or a pseudonym.

Because of the number of different contributions and contributors in each book, there is no payment though I'm afraid. Nor can I send a complimentary copy out to everyone either; because of the number of different contributors and countries represented in each book, it would just be far too expensive. However I will send all contributors a pdf copy, and all our books will be available at very competitive prices from thirteen Amazon websites worldwide, as both a larger format (6 inch x 9 inch or 15.24 cm x 22.86 cm) paperback and Kindle.

If you are interested in seeing your work published, and your words read, please send your contribution/s with the name of the Collection in the subject line, along with a brief writers' biography (100 - 200 words plus any contact details you want publishing e.g. your website, email, blog etc. plus your nationality and the country where you are currently based) to me to:

E: Editor@collectionsofpoetryandprose.com

If you love writing, wherever you are in the world, whatever your experience of writing, please do contribute!

Our next collection:
LOVE - A Collection of Poetry and Prose on Loving and Being in Love

Followed by:
- TRAVEL - A Collection of Poetry and Prose on Travels and Travelling.
- HAPPY - A Collection of Poetry and Prose on Happiness and Being Happy
- WAR - A Collection of Poetry and Prose about both the Bravery and Horror of War

You can submit to multiple Collections, and up to six pieces per Collection too! go to: CollectionsofPoetryandProse.com

Other Collections...

Poetic Bahrain: A collection of contemporary poetry about the Kingdom of Bahrain
Compiled by Robin Barratt
Forty-seven poems by twenty-five poets from ten countries, Poetic Bahrain is a wonderful, unique and eclectic mixture of both traditional and modern verse, focusing on Bahrain; its people, its culture and its way of life. A must read if you love Bahrain and you love poetry.
Paperback - ISBN: 978-1511429290
Kindle - ASIN: B00WIMBD2W

My Beautiful Bahrain: A collection of short stories and poetry about life and living in the Kingdom of Bahrain.
Compiled by Robin Barratt
Bahrain's beauty is not aesthetic, it is not visual - its beauty is much deeper, hidden, and much more personal. In this way, and to many people, Bahrain is beautiful. And, as many of the stories in this book will demonstrate, Bahrain's beauty is fundamentally the subtle, gentle beauty of the island, its way of life and the friendliness, compassion, openness and warmth of its people. With lots of fascinating personal 'life' stories, quite a few tourist-type information and fact based contributions, some wonderful poetry, an occasional piece of fiction (set on the island) and a mixture of other diverse and captivating prose, with fifty contributions from forty writers from fifteen countries, My Beautiful Bahrain is both varied and unique, and an undeniably indispensable guide for travellers and visitors to the island, as well as a 'must-read' book for people living here, doing business here, or just interested in what life is like living on this tiny, tiny island in the Arabian Gulf.
Paperback – ISBN: 978-1507774427
Kindle - ASIN: B0076WJSJY

More of My Beautiful Bahrain: More short stories and poetry about life and living in the Kingdom of Bahrain
Compiled by Robin Barratt
Following on from My Beautiful Bahrain, written by both locals and expats with fascinating personal 'life' stories, tourist-type information and fact based contributions, some wonderful poetry and compelling fiction (set in the Kingdom), More of My Beautiful Bahrain is another varied and unique collection of short stories and poetry about life and living on this tiny little island in the Arabian Sea. Twenty-seven chapters by 24 writers including; English, Irish, American, Canadian, Pakistani, Indian, Palestinian, Kuwaiti, Australian, Nepalese, Yemeni

and German, with contributions from Bahraini writers too, this is a must-read for travellers and visitors to the island, as well as for people moving there, living there, doing business there, or just interested in what life is like there.
Paperback – ISBN: 978-1507681312
Kindle - ASIN: B00PMBIG4O

Waiting Spaces: A collection of poems describing our life's thoughts, feelings and experiences
By David Hollywood
A wonderful eclectic collection of almost 80 poems by Bahrain's esteemed poet David Hollywood. David, originally from Ireland but now a resident of the Kingdom of Bahrain, is jointly responsible for the Bahrain Writers' Circle, now one of the biggest multi-national clubs for writers across the region, The Second Circle, Bahrain's biggest multi-national poetry group, and organises the annual The Colours of Life Poetry Festival. one of the most important culturally cosmopolitan events to take place within all of The Gulf region. A must read if you love poetry and love the wonderful eccentricity that is sometimes David Hollywood.
Paperback - ISBN: 978-1507633076
Kindle - ASIN: B00OJA5JJY

www.CollectionsofPoetryandProse.com

Printed in Great Britain
by Amazon